Planning Your High School Reunion

Rhonda Teel
Kimberly McElliott

Montage Publishing
Kirkland, Washington

Montage Publishing
13501 100th Avenue N.E., Suite 5047
Kirkland, WA 98034

Dedication

To my son Griffin, who reminds me daily that our life here should be spent loving everyone.

And for Kim Grant, whose patience, understanding and friendship goes unsurpassed and without whom there would have never been any reunions.

Lastly, to J.J., who allowed me to spend a year of my life in Camelot.

R.T.

To my husband, Tim, who listened to my "idea," took a deep breath, and kept me laughing while it became a reality. All my love always.

And to my parents from whom I inherited perseverance. I needed it! Thank you for your ongoing support.

K.M.F.

Acknowledgments

To all the creative, energetic and committed Reunion Committees I've worked with, who make my job my passion, Gary McCormick, Pat Keogh, Nori Patrick, Jodi Palmblade, Lynn Smith, Roxanne Kubicek, Carlton Lockwood, Wendy Greene, Ellen Sandler, Nancy Garvey, Dan Clancy and Andrea.

R.T.

Special thanks to Jim Vlassis, my high school principal, an exceptional person who understands that high school should be memorable.

And to Mike DeRisi, my class advisor, who had the dedication and foresight to know that a reunion is one way to keep memories alive.

K.M.F.

Table of Contents

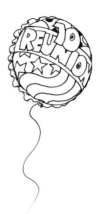

Introduction

~ ~

A high school reunion is the next best thing after the senior prom — may be even better. Years will have passed since graduation and the majority of the classmates will not have seen each for a long time. Perhaps only a few have stayed in touch with each other. The promise of getting together, catching up, renewing old friendships, congratulating each other for achieving goals, celebrating successes and sharing life's experiences is a most appealing idea and fills the heart with anticipation.

It's also an event both planners and participants are awaiting eagerly, and are able to enjoy together. All through the planning process, the members of the these tasks to make the process more manageable. You will have fun, save time, and the end results will spell *success.*

As I mentioned earlier, this is one occasion where planners and attendees profit equally from the outcome — everyone is rewarded with a memory-making event that reunites old friends and strengthens the bonds made years ago. Just think how much fun *you* are going to have reminiscing about your high school days while you and your committee work on the plans for your reunion.

And, with the help of this book, the event will linger and last months instead of just one night!

Go ahead, everybody — have fun!

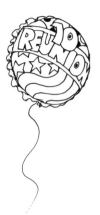

1 - A Tradition Is Born

~ ~

It all started with the first graduating class and a group of young people who grew up together and became "forever-friends." They were classroom buddies, flirted, had their first crushes, worried about the future, shared secrets, cheered at football games, stewed about grades, fretted about looks, traded books, haunted malls and pizza parlors, rocked out to the same tunes, partied, discussed the state of the world as well as their own hopes and dreams, and wanted to relive the good old days with their high school classmates at a festive gathering.

Nostalgia and memories gave birth to the first high school reunion. Ever since then, the event has grown in

~ ~

popularity and has become a time-honored tradition for countless people. Each year, Americans come from every corner of the country — or from just across town — to touch base again with familiar faces, hug old friends, gossip, share their new lives, and have a heck of a lot of fun. People remember the date of their high school reunion from the moment they receive that first announcement in the mail.

They stick that flyer on the refrigerator, circle the date on their calendars, and make plans to attend. They organize their activities around that important date — leave the kids with grandparents, put the dog in the kennel, shop for that perfect party get-up, and pack their bags. They travel by car or by plane — and they get there full of anticipation and good cheer because they're going to have a terrific time!

High school reunions are popular because they offer something for everyone. Some will find great joy in reacquainting themselves with old friends, others relish reminiscing about the events that shaped and highlighted the era in which they attended high school. Some may even find a new romance. What ever the individual experiences may be, everybody loves that touch of nostalgia — looking back wistfully to that time that was so important, so dramatic and sometimes so devastating. It is amazing how much better things look after the generous passage of time. How wonderful it is that reunions offer an opportunity to touch the past without reliving it.

Attending a high school reunion can be quite an emotional experience for the participants. People don't base

~ ~

their decision whether to attend or stay away on the cost of the trip, the time, place or distance — they come to reunions to rediscover friendship. Attending school, having been together for years before going out into the big world, and having shared so many things creates strong bonds that last. Taking part in the process of reunion planning is a great way to extend the trip down memory lane for the committee members.

Some classes opt for planning the upcoming reunion themselves with the help of committees, while others may choose to hire a class reunion planning company as an alternative. Some reunion committees are unable to devote the time necessary to attend to every detail for the event and rely on the expertise of established reunion companies. These professionals assume responsibility for the up-front costs, handle the administrative duties, and, with input from the committee, coordinate all aspects of the reunion.

While reunion specialists can save you time and do the work for you, it does not eliminate the need for a reunion committee. With the help of a reunion company, members of the committee can choose just how involved they want to become and which of the tasks (if any) they will do themselves. Remember that the success of the event depends on everyone working together.

Look in your telephone directory for reunion planners. Be sure to interview a few companies and compare notes on costs, services, and quality of mailing materials.

~ ~

Questions to Ask a Reunion Planning Company

1. How long have you been in business?
2. How many reunions do you organize per year?
3. Can we see samples of your mailers, memory books and name badges?
4. How flexible are you regarding locations?
5. How involved can the committee be in the planning?
6. Do you have different mailer styles to select from?
7. Do you provide the committee with updates regarding their reunion plans?
8. Is your staff available to answer questions?
9. May I see photos from reunion parties you have done?
10. Do you have references?
11. What search methods do you use?
12. Are you insured and bonded?
13. What is your fee?

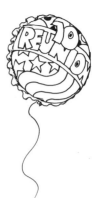

2 - Senior Class Councils and Advisors

~ ~

Last spring, I attended a high school senior class council meeting with the intention of discussing their first reunion. Not surprisingly, I was met with a few blank stares, puzzled expressions, and several comments like, "We haven't even graduated yet, how can we think about our reunion?" If it hadn't been for my senior class advisor, I probably would have reacted just like that. Fortunately, he had the foresight to discuss our 10-year reunion as part of things-to-do while we were still in school, and we all had a good notion of what details and effort would go into "reunion-making."

~ ~

When I started planning my 10-year reunion, I was armed with a reunion fund, two sets of our class list, a slide show and our time-capsule filled with high-school-days memorabilia. I definitely had a head start for directing the process flow. But, even so, our committee dedicated a lot of time and energy in planning the event.

Very few committees are ahead of the game when it comes time to plan their reunion. Ironically, planners could have saved themselves time and money had they made just a few simple arrangements prior to their graduation.

Here Are Some Things You Can Do Your Senior Year

1. Gather your class list prior to graduation and distribute the list to one or two council members. It will be their responsibility to contact the high school eight or nine years later when it's time to organize the reunion committee.

2. Hire a tracking service. Having help from a tracking service is one of the best gifts a class can give itself. Several tracking services like Reunion Resource in Redlands, California, have emerged to cater to high school graduating classes. These companies take your class list and keep track of your classmates for at least five years — constantly updating the list and providing summaries to the class contact person. Working with a tracking service is worth its weight in gold.

~ ~

Since most of the up-front expenses in planning a reunion are incurred in searching for classmates, you are saving yourselves phone, mailing and research costs by having access to updated addresses when the planning begins. These immediate savings will in turn reduce your ticket price. And, best of all, sending invitations to accurate addresses will increase the attendance at the event.

Reunion Resource charges $1 per classmate per year of tracking. The company tracks nationwide and can be reached at 800-315-3577.

3. Time-capsule. Purchase a trunk or box that can be locked for your time-capsule. Let seniors know that you want them to leave a memory in the time-capsule. Our time-capsule was filled with anything from notes, pompoms, envelopes of photos to personal awards. The capsule is to be locked upon graduation and re-opened at the reunion! The contents of the time capsule make an ideal display for the event, and I guarantee its contents will jog a few memories and pull a few heartstrings!

4. Slide show. In case you prepare a slide show or videotape of Senior Week events, don't forget to save it for the reunion. If there is special music that accompanies it, make sure it is saved as well. The slide show is one of the highlights of a high school reunion.

5. Senior will and predictions. Ask your classmates to pre-
    pare wills and/or predictions for the future. Senior wills
    typically include the "passing on" of lockers, parking
    spaces and favorite spots in the lunchroom to under-
    classmen. These are fun to read much later on. Senior
    predictions for the future are especially entertaining ten
    years later. What do your classmates think they'll be
    doing in ten years? Where do they think they'll be
    living and working? Even if you don't share them with
    the group, the authors will have fun reading them at
    the reunion.

    *My time-capsule included a few predictions, but the
    most creative prediction was from a group of friends
    from a history class. Six classmates made some pre-
    dictions about each other, with a special commentary
    on how their romantic lives would be. I can't confirm
    how accurate they were, but the friends spent a signif-
    icant amount of time huddled in the corner reminiscing
    over their predictions for one another.*

6. Reunion fund. The up-front expenses for planning a
    reunion will amount to approximately $1,500, to
    include:

    • Deposits for hotel accommodations.
    • Deposits for a disc jockey or a band.
    • Postage and printing cost for announcement
       flyers.

At times, a senior class has some money left after graduation as a result of vendor rebates or budget management by a frugal class council. Ideally, the extra money should go into a "Reunion Fund" for future reunion planning. If possible, the class should open a non-interest, two-signatures bearing account (unless you want to pay taxes on it.) However, this could be a sticky issue in some schools. There are districts which do not allow classes to take the money with them when they graduate. Check into your school district's policy. If they do not permit you to have a "Reunion Fund," consider using the remaining money to hire a tracking service before you graduate. It will be money well spent.

It's always good to know what to expect. As my English professor used to say, "Forewarned is forearmed." Be ready! Good luck!

3 - Background on Reunions

~ ~

The phenomenon of the high school reunion lies in the questions … "I wonder what happened to so-and-so? I wonder what so-and-so looks like now? I wonder if so-and-so ever married so-and-so? I wonder ... I wonder ... I wonder ...?"

Perfectly normal curiosity and a deep sense of nostalgia make reunions enticing, and as the reunion coordinator, you know the feeling well. Perhaps it started when you dusted off your yearbook only to realize hours later that you had flipped through the whole thing. Or maybe you heard through the grapevine that your high school sweetheart was getting married and a whole barrage of memories washed over you.

Whatever triggered your thoughts, it was your curiosity, excitement and initiative that ultimately led you to this book. *Planning Your High School Reunion* offers you manageable guidelines and new ideas for planning your reunion. Let it be your guide through the many tasks that lie ahead for you and have double the fun!

Start-up Chores

1. As the reunion coordinator, notify the high school and local newspapers about the upcoming event and let them know that all inquiries are to be directed to you.

   Your first call is to your high school where you should register your name as the reunion coordinator and leave your name and telephone number. If there is someone who has already volunteered for the job, get in touch with that person and discuss your roles. If two groups have started planning the event, it is best to merge the groups and start over. Two heads may be better than one, but two groups planning the same reunion independently of each other are headed for disaster. That's exactly what happened not long ago at one high school:

   Redlands High School Class of 1977 had quite a dilemma when it was discovered that two different committees were planning the 10-year reunion. Two separate committees had selected different locations, dates and vendors before they realized the problem.

~ ~

Human nature being what it is, the two groups had difficulty reaching a mutually satisfactory decision. There were many classmates who elected not to attend the reunion after learning of the feud and the committees' inability to work together. The committee with the most people prevailed, but not without alienating a lot of people. This reunion could have been a total disaster. As it was, it left a lot of individuals bruised and disappointed and may have easily lent a sour note to the festivities.

Some high schools predetermine the reunion coordinator. Sometimes the job goes to the Senior Class President or the Associated Student Body President. However, the task of reunion coordinator *should* go to the person who really wants to do the job.

2. Request a copy of the senior class list from the registrar. Accept all the information that is being given to you.

   Some schools keep records of all incoming inquiries for an upcoming reunion. Ask the person at the front desk for updated addresses and other pertinent information she may have. You may be pleasantly surprised to know that a school staff member is responsible for all reunion inquiries, and is required to keep track of them. You may want to give the school several self-addressed, stamped envelopes and ask the staff to mail you the new addresses and information collected. This person will be helpful throughout the planning process. Make sure to leave your name and phone number so the front desk can pass it along to inquiring classmates.

~ ~

Note: Some schools will not release the class list to you for various reasons — due to the Privacy Act, or because the list has been lost. If that is the case with your class list, don't despair. See Chapter 8, *Searching for Classmates*, "Starting from Scratch/No Class List Available" Section.

3. Form a committee. By registering your name with the school, you may get calls from class members who want to be active in the planning process. Also, try to reach people from the senior class council or other school groups, such as the National Honor Society, the school paper, or members of the band. These classmates showed a special interest in being involved in high school activities and are probably most willing to do their part to get the ball rolling. Get in touch with them and ask for volunteers.

To refresh your memory, look through your yearbook. Solicit help from classmates with whom you've stayed in touch, or place an announcement in the local paper about your intentions of forming a planning committee. Such an announcement may qualify as a public service announcement (PSA), which is of no cost to you, appears in a special section of the newspaper, and can run for up to one year. Call your local paper for detailed information (see Sample Letter Format on next page).

~ ~

Sample Letter Format for Newspapers and Radio/TV Stations

_____High School Reunion
(Name of city where school is located)
Reunion Committee of 19____ Class
Sharon Jones – Chairman
15571 Orange Road
Los Angeles, CA 90010

Attention: Public Service Announcement Editor

The enclosed Press Release is self-explanatory.
At your earliest convenience, would you please
have this announcement inserted within the
proper section so we may locate more of our
classmates? The date of our reunion will be
(month, day, year).

Yours truly,

Sharon Jones
(Phone Number)

Enclosure:
Press Release

Press Release

The 19____ graduating class of
_____ High School in (name of
city) is holding its ____th year reunion on
(month, day, year) at (location). Please contact
(name) at (phone number) for details.

~ ~

Look for diversity on your committee. You'll be amazed how much more you'll have in common with your classmates now than ever before. Everybody will have done a lot of growing and changing — time does wonders to all of us. Also, a committee that includes classmates from all the different high school factions appeals to a wider audience. By including a variety of people on your committee, you are attracting people from a variety of backgrounds and interests. As a result, more people will attend the reunion. The goal is to get the whole senior class if possible! If they can identify with the people who are planning their reunion, they'll get even more excited about coming to the party. (See Chapter 4, *The Reunion Committee,* for more information.)

Consider asking members of the graduating classes immediately before and after yours to join your committee. Members of the class before you can walk you through their successes and failures and save you all sorts of grief. Those who are a year behind will be interested in benefitting from your experience when they do their reunion next year.

4. Determine the lead time you need. Depending upon the size of your class, the search for class members should begin eight to eighteen months before the event. For classes of less than 500 students, eight months is a sufficient time span. For larger classes, devote more

~ ~

time to the process — ideally, 12 months, and consider getting out multiple mailings. The earlier you start, the more time you have to find all your classmates. After you have determined how much lead time it will take, set up your first committee meeting.

5. Schedule your first meeting. Allow enough time to cover the agenda items and spend the rest of meeting just reminiscing about your high school days. Enthusiasm breeds enthusiasm.

     You have a great opportunity to start your reunion planning off on the right foot. For the sake of efficiency, some people may suggest you to keep this meeting "all business" — but we say, "Reminisce!" Remember when … remember who … remember what and how? That kind of conversation, recalling names and faces and incidents — especially the funny ones — sets the mood, kindles the energy and enthusiasm for your committee to get things done.

     Since nostalgia reigns supreme for this undertaking, bring out some high school memorabilia, talk about Mr. Jones, the history teacher, the time the cafeteria served soup in juice glasses, and the day someone hid the cheerleaders uniforms just before the big game. Consider this the first reunion of many more to follow, so pave the way and let the fun begin! (See Chapter 5, *Getting Started: Meeting #1.*)

~ ~

Off-Year Reunions

For the more ambitious committees, holding a reunion every five years doesn't seem too intimidating. Although 5-, 15- and 25-year reunions remain popular, they differ slightly from the traditional 10-, 20- and 30-year events.

The characteristics of an "off-year" reunion are::

1. They *usually* have a smaller turnout.
2. They *should* cost less.
3. They should be different; perhaps a theme party or casual event.
4. But — they're just as much fun.

By definition, a reunion is a fun and nostalgic event that attracts a crowd every time. Depending on how many classmates still live in town, you could have quite a turnout.

We suggest that you keep your ticket price down for an off-year reunion. You do this by using a less elaborate facility, creating a directory instead of a memory book, and not offering formal photographs. Try to keep the price at $30 or less per person, and you will entice many classmates.

While the event may not be as elaborate as the traditional reunion, the off-year reunion presents an opportunity to update classmates' names and addresses. Gather this information diligently, since it will be valuable to the next reunion committee. (See Chapter 8, *Searching for Classmates,* for tips on how to locate classmates.)

~ ~

Sometimes a less elaborate and less costly event is more inviting to some classmates. You may have guests at an off-year reunion who wouldn't attend the big 10- or 20-year bash. The goal is to get people reunited, so don't think you have to plan a big party every time.

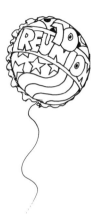

4 - The Reunion Committee

~ ~

You and your committee have embarked on an important task. Because of you, your classmates will have the opportunity to step back into the past for a few hours, catch up to the present with old and new friends, and take home a suitcase full of new memories. They will have enjoyed themselves immensely and, even though it's a long time away, they will probably not think twice about attending the next reunion.

To maximize your enjoyment throughout the planning, emphasize *fun* and relish the time you are spending with your classmates. Like any team, you must work together throughout the planning process. All the effort that goes into the careful planning will be reflected in the event.

~ ~

Here are some hints regarding the dynamics of your reunion committee:

1. Take the time to get reacquainted. If you get side-tracked with some reminiscing, don't worry about it! After all, you are planning a reunion, and that's part of it. In fact, the planning stages can offer great rewards. *We've heard that during the planning stages of the Redlands High School Class of 1963 Twenty-Year Reunion, two classmates, Gary McCormick and Maggie Barrett, became reacquainted while working on the reunion committee. Their newly-found friendship blossomed into romance while they helped plan their high school reunion. For a happy ending to the story, they were married shortly after the reunion — and live happily ever after.*

   Mary Fairchild in Seattle, Washington, confessed that she joined the planning committee for her 10-year reunion at the very last moment. She had no intention of attending her reunion, but after getting reacquainted with the committee members and enjoying the planning process, she decided it would really be fun to attend the event. She went to all the functions — solo — visited with just about everyone, had a wonderful time and was asked out by three former classmates.

   There are many stories floating around about some of the wonderful things that happened to classmates as a direct result of being involved in reunion activities. Reunions result in of a lot of fun happenings.

~ ~

2. Select one person to be the committee leader. This person schedules and leads the meetings, oversees the various sub-committees and acts as the point person for all members. In most instances, decisions will be made as a group. However, if an executive decision is needed, the committee leader takes responsibility. All deadlines and budgets are to be monitored by the committee leader.

3. Committees do not need the entire class' input before making decisions. Point of fact: if your classmates really wanted to have their say, they would be working on the committee.

4. Planning should be fun too! Don't get bogged down by tough decisions. Use the majority vote system in decision making.

5. By breaking into sub-committees, each member has a greater voice on his project. Sub-committees should not have to present every decision to the entire group.

6. Remember, not everyone will have the same amount of time to devote to the planning stages. That's all right — there are big tasks and little tasks to be completed. Ask the committee members to determine the amount of time they can volunteer and delegate the tasks accordingly.

~ ~

7. Reward yourselves! Does your hotel offer a complimentary room? Raffle it off to a committee member or use it for holding a reunion pre-party for the committee.

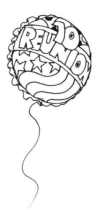

5 - Getting Started: Meeting #1

~ ~

Goals

- Discuss the nature of the event: activities all weekend? picnics? theme party?
- Determine the month for the event and select options for the facility.
- Set up a reunion committee meeting schedule.

Nature of Event

Theme

After you have chosen your theme, you will discover the many ways to tie in the theme to your reunion party. If you have a site that has a specific theme of its own, incorporate it into your invitations, your printed materials, and decorations.

For example, a popular event site in downtown Seattle, Washington, is the General Petroleum Museum, which is a converted warehouse loft exhibiting showpieces of antique petroleum and gas station memorabilia. Surrounded by a priceless collection of gas pumps and artifacts from the early part of the century, it easily makes a great site for a "Blast to the Past" theme.

Another example is the Stephen/Burke Aquarium in La Jolla, California. Set atop the cliffs of La Jolla with a spectacular view of the Pacific, this functioning aquarium is available for events in the evenings. Guests are allowed to roam the aquarium, mingle at the edge of tide pools and enjoy the view. This facility lends itself to nautical or luau themes.

Other themes which have become increasingly popular are: Country Western, Black & White, Mystery, Big-Top Sock Hop, 70s Disco Fever, or 60s Motown. Banquet rooms are ideal places for transformation to represent a specific theme. Many hotels have backdrops and decorations available to be rented for the occasion. Just ask the catering department.

~ ~

Weekend Event

The number one complaint at most reunions is that *it went by too fast!* The old saying holds true: "My, how time flies when you're having fun." You have the opportunity to plan a variety of events — s-t-r-e-t-c-h time and make the reunion last longer by offering additional activities.

Some committees plan additional activities that cater to families or offer events in a variety of settings to reunite classmates. The budget won't be affected because, in most cases, the guests pay for these activities separately.

By offering additional gatherings, classmates can spend more time with each other and catch up with more old friends. Activities like a Friday night cocktail party, Sunday afternoon picnic, a sports tournament or a brunch offer an opportunity for classmates to meet in more casual settings which tend to be less cost restrictive than the big reunion party.

How ambitious is your committee? If a variety of activities sound like fun and are realistic goals for your committee to complete, delegate the tasks immediately.

Selecting the Facility

Select a Site Coordinator

The decision of where the event is to take place will have the biggest effect on your budget. Facilities range from high school gymnasiums to hotel ballrooms. Most cities have a good selection of places which lend

~ ~

themselves well to accommodating a reunion. To begin with, consider the size of your reunion party. The Reunion Company in Redlands, California, suggests that you use a 35 percent attendance estimate as a safe guideline. After organizing over 100 reunions for classes of all sizes, they have found that approximately 30 to 35 percent of the total class attends a reunion. (That figure includes dates and spouses).

If you have a class of 400 graduates, plan on 120 to 160 guests to attend your reunion party. Remember, the sooner you begin searching for classmates, the higher the attendance percentage. Good sources to lead you to event location sites are the local Chamber of Commerce, Yellow Pages®, or better yet, a local wedding directory, bridal magazine, or friends.

Hotels offer a large variety of full-service options for reunions and are usually the most flexible about accommodating those extra people who decide to show up at the last minute and expect to be squeezed right in without ruffling feathers.

If you anticipate a good number of out-of-town guests, a convenient location is important. Usually, hotels qualify for easy accessibility and satisfactory parking facilities. Most major hotels have catering services, offer group room rates, floral amenities, audio/visual equipment and sometimes have theme decoration materials available.

Contrary to popular belief, it is usually not less expensive to plan an event in a location where you have to arrange for outside services such as food and beverage catering, the renting of table linens, and decorations.

~ ~

Even though a hotel may offer the most complete accommodations and readily available services, don't discount the use of museums, ranches, country clubs, aquariums, marinas, mansions and wineries for alternative event sites. These sites offer unique settings and come complete with an inherent theme you can expand on successfully. It is not unusual for the site to have an event coordinator or an in-house catering department which can handle your event requirements as easily as any hotel.

The more desirable the location of the facility — waterfront, downtown, etc. — the higher the expenses. Don't let this deter you from selecting a prime location, just be sure to do your homework first. A good measure for determining the cost of a facility is to ask the banquet manager for the "average price per person for food" (buffet and sit-down). The largest portion of your overall ticket price is spent on food. If the facility charges, on average, $30 per person for food — your ticket price jumps to nearly $60 when you tack on the other expenses. Be sure to include tax and gratuities, usually 22 percent.

There are exceptions to the rule, however. Some facilities waive the room fee or include linens and other amenities in the cost of the food.

Always know what is included in the prices quoted you.

Ask questions and make sure that you fully understand just what you get for your money.

Look for hidden costs (taxes and gratuities) and make sure you have all charges itemized and submitted in writing.

~ ~

One way to gauge the cost of using a hotel (in addition to the expenses for food) is to inquire about the group rates for sleeping rooms. If the group rate is more than what the majority of your committee wants to pay, then you might get your class in over its head. It's not uncommon for prime location hotels to have unusually high rates and a very limited off-peak season.

I recall the quote my committee received when we were looking for a location for our 10-year reunion. I had my heart set on using a waterfront hotel in San Diego because of its attractive location and ambiance. When we checked out the costs, we learned that the food cost came to $40 per person and the group rates for rooms were $139 per night.

Time out for a reality check!

Unlike weddings, bar mitzvahs or conventions, reunion guests pay for all of the expenses of the event through the ticket price. If you have to choose between keeping the costs affordable and a ritzy location — remember, it is more important to have a good turnout than a great view. Looking into the friendly, laughing faces of old buddies is more important than looking at the scenery.

Delegate the task of finding location options to the site coordinator immediately. Armed with the date and a list of location ideas, this volunteer is responsible for investigating all the possibilities for a suitable location. As a committee, set a deadline date for the site coordinator's findings so a final decision can be reached.

~ ~

Committee Questions

Here are some questions the committee will have to decide on early in the planning sessions:

1. Facility ideas and suggestions: Hotel? Museum? Mansion?
2. Will it be a buffet or a sit-down dinner?
3. Will we have cocktails and hors d'oeuvres during check-in?
4. What time of the year will it be?

Hints

Reunions typically offer sit-down dinners. People tend to look at a buffet dinner more like a generous spread of hors d'oeuvres and prefer to sit down and be served. Your classmates may feel like they are getting more "bang for their buck" with a sit-down dinner. Buffets often cost approximately $5 per person more than a sit-down dinner. No matter whether you are having a buffet or a sit-down dinner, always allow for at least 20 to 30 *walk-up* guests.

Be realistic about the number of guests you are expecting. As we mentioned before, estimate the number of attendees based on 30-35 percent of the size of your class. It is important that you come as close as possible to the number of guests expected when you order food, because you have to pay for the number of dinners you guaranteed to the caterer regardless of a smaller turnout.

Another good thing to know is that it takes at least one hour to check in your guests (depending on the size of the group).

Therefore, to make the check-in enjoyable and fun, designate that time as cocktail hour and give your guests the opportunity mingle and catch up with each other until everyone has been checked in. Cocktail hours make the check-in a social gathering rather than a tedious, waiting-in-line chore.

Questions to Ask Before Selecting a Facility

On the next two pages is a list of questions for the site coordinator to ask facility managers before selecting your location.

After selecting the facility, the site coordinator has a lot of things to arrange, including making sure the facility manager answers all his questions satisfactorily. Ask the facility manager to put **EVERYTHING** in writing. Review the agreement carefully, and sign only when all items are the way you want them.

~ ~

Questions to Ask Before Selecting a Facility

1. What is the average cost per person for food, including taxes and gratuities? (Tax and gratuity are frequently overlooked when getting price quotes. Neglecting to figure these in could cause you to lose money.)
   Buffet dinner $_____ Sit-down dinner $_____
2. Can you accommodate all of the guests comfortably (buffet or sit-down)?
3. How will the tables be set up? May I see a sample table layout for a party the size of ours?
4. Is there a different area — a foyer, patio or breezeway — to hold the cocktail hour?
5. May I see photos of similar occasions held at your facility?
6. Are parking facilities adequate for our size group?
   Is there handicapped parking?
   Is guest parking free of charge?
7. Are there adequate restrooms?
8. How big is the dance floor?
9. Is there a public address system?
10. Are there enough electrical outlets for projectors, microphones, memorabilia display, etc.
11. Do you have audio/visual equipment available?
    Do you charge a rental fee?
    Do you have staff to set it up?
    Will staff be available if we have problems?

~ ~

Questions to Ask Before Selecting a Facility (cont'd.)

12. Do you offer in-house catering?
    What is the deadline for calling in the final head count?
    How do you staff the event?
13. Can you accommodate extra dinner guests?
    If so, how many?
14. When may we arrive to set up?
15. What is the established shutdown time?
    Can we pay for overtime if necessary?
    What is the hourly charge?
16. Who is responsible for cleanup?
17. Will vendors be able to make deliveries at the facility on the day of the event?
18. How do we confirm our date?
19. Is the deposit negotiable?
20. When is balance due?
21. What is your cancellation policy?
22. Whom do I see about group sleeping room rates?
23. Is there a charge for the banquet room/ballroom — or is it included in the food cost?
24. Are there any limitations on decorating the room?
25. What decorations or backdrops do you have available?
26. What do you have to offer for table set-ups?
    What colors are your table linens?

~ ~

Menu

Discuss the basic menu with your committee and decide what to offer as the main course. Or will you offer a buffet? When you plan a sit-down dinner with entrée options, your classmates will have to make their dinner selections ahead of time. If you choose to offer menu options, the selection must appear on the reservation form in the invitation. The site coordinator may have to make independent decisions on a few items, but as a whole, you should let the members of the committee voice their preferences. The facility manager will be able to make recommendations as well. Be sure to ask him if the kitchen is able to accommodate special requests, such as a vegetarian dinner. Bear in mind that special requests and split menus (two entrée options) may cost more.

Currently, a popular set-up for dinner is "stations." Stations are individual tables set up throughout the room with one particular theme or entrée. Many facilities offer this set-up because it enables guests to mingle and dine at their leisure — or simultaneously — thus eliminating the classic congestion of a buffet line.

Alternatively, the sit-down dinner is indeed more formal. And, as we mentioned, it is perceived to offer more "bang for the buck." If you are planning on making a lot of announcements or have entertainment during the dinner hour, you may prefer to have a more captive audience of seated guests. In making menu and dinner set-up selections, consider the advantages of both and assess the personality of your class before you decide.

~ ~

Hint

Don't expect to get a unanimous vote from your committee. If appropriate, get the opinions of a few people and make an executive decision.

On the following two pages are menu ideas for 1) dinner buffet, 2) sit-down dinner and 3) dinner stations, as developed by the U.S. Grant Hotel in San Diego, CA.

A friend of mine gave me an idea for a menu item that would be fun to serve at our high school reunion dinner. Peanut Butter Chews — a wonderful culinary experience, basically a peanut butter brownie, was a popular dessert in our school cafeteria. Hundreds of these chewy bars were sold daily. My friend was so enamored with these goodies that she coaxed the recipe out of one of the cooks and offered it for use at our reunion. The hotel chef was willing to to make them, and we were in business.

We set up a separate dessert table in the dining room following the meal, and served coffee and Peanut Butter Chews (they were just as delicious as I remembered) to the delight of our classmates.

~ ~

Sample Menus

Dinner Buffet Menu

Mixed Green Salad with Citrus Segments
Spinach and Mushroom Salad
Pasta Salad

Chicken Breasts with Basil Cream Sauce
Carved Steamship Round of Beef

Long Grain Wild Rice
Baby Russets with Cilantro Butter
Fresh Season Vegetables

Dessert: Assorted Cakes, Pies, Pastries

Sit-Down Dinner Menu

Caesar Salad
Chicken with Basil Cream Sauce
Rice or Potato
Seasonal Vegetables
Bread Item
Chocolate Cake or Raspberry Mirror

~ ~

Sample Menus

Dinner Station Menu

Pasta Station
Server to Prepare
Tortellini with White Wine Cream Sauce
Linguini with Clam Sauce and Bow Tie Pasta With
Marinara Sauce
Condiments and Garlic Bread

Carving Station
Roasted Steamboat Round of Beef
Honey Bourbon Glazed Ham
Horseradish, Grain and Traditional Mustards
Mayonnaise and Petite Rolls

Fruit and Cheese Station
Fress Sliced Fruit
Imported and Domestic Cheeses
English Crackers and Sliced French Bread

Fajita Station
Beef or Chicken Fajitas
Tortillas, Salsa, Onions, Cheese
Guacamole and Jalapeños

Dessert Station
Apple Strudel with Brandied Vanilla Sauce
Assortment of Mini-Pastries, Cheesecake
Sacher Torte, Black Forest Cake

~ ~

Decor

1. Ask the facility manager what color tablecloths and napkins are available.
2. Inquire if the check-in and memorabilia tables come with skirting. If skirting is a separate item, make sure the request is noted.
3. What do the place settings look like? (Make sure the china is in good condition.)
4. What decorations are available?
5. If you have decided to serve a dinner buffet, ask what the hotel's buffet decorations look like, and ask to see pictures of a full buffet and to see how the food is presented.

Room Layout and Set-Up

How will the room be designed?

Keep in my mind how you want the traffic to flow. Ideally, check-in and formal photo sessions should take place in the foyer or another nearby room if available.

Also consider where you want the slide show to be in relation to the table set up. Make sure all the guests will have a clear view for viewing the program.

If you plan to have a memorabilia display, select an area that will not interfere with dining or the program. Some facilities can provide easels or backdrops for your memorabilia display. Ask the facility to set them up with the room set-up.

~ ~

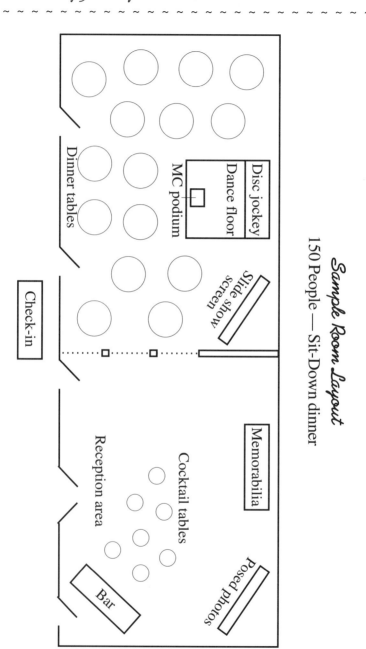

Sample Room Layout
150 People — Sit-Down dinner

~ ~

Typically, the facility manager will want to design the layout. Carefully inform him of your special needs and ask for a diagram after the design is complete. You should offer your suggestions, but rely on his expertise as well. (See the Sample Room Layout on the previous page.)

Other Questions to Ask Your Facility Manager

- What time will the room be set up?
- Will the tables have tablecloths, skirting or placemats?
- Will outside vendors or committee members be able to set up at the same time?

Event Date

The time from May through October is the most popular time for holding reunions. Most committees feel compelled to hold their reunion around the time they graduated, which is May or June. But, depending on where you live, this may not be the most ideal time. Consider dates from an adult perspective. Many class members may have school-age children, or perhaps the weather isn't conducive to travel during a particular month. If you are planning a whole weekend of activities, in which children are encouraged to attend, consider a time when families can take a vacation together.

Some high schools, like the Palm Spring High School Class of 1983, organize their reunion dates around the school's homecoming game. PSHS 1983 alumni attended the homecoming football game, which was followed by a fun welcome party on the Friday night before the reunion

~ ~

dinner. *What a great idea to break the ice before the big event — especially for those who are returning to their old stomping grounds for the first time in 10 years!*

It is important to remember that, as long as you give your classmates enough time to plan to attend their reunion, they will come. If the time frame is narrow, people may feel pushed into making a decision and end up declining to participate in the event.

Choose several possible dates for the reunion in order to have flexibility in selecting a facility, and give this information to the site coordinator.

Setting Up the Reunion Committee Meeting Schedule

We recommend that the entire committee meets once a month during the beginning stages of planning. Pick a specific day of the week to meet — say, the first Tuesday of every month. This way people can reserve that day for the months ahead. Better yet, prepare a schedule to hand out to everyone listing the meeting dates. It is very important that the entire committee attends the planning meetings regularly to keep abreast of the progress and to do their share of the work.

When the time draws closer to the event — approximately three to four months — the committee should meet at least twice a month to ensure that they take care of all details. Sub-committees should have their own separate meetings.

Meeting #1 in Review

1. What is the theme of the party?
2. Will there be additional events?
   If yes, who will organize these events?
   What is the deadline for volunteers to submit ideas for additional weekend events?
3. Who is the site coordinator?
4. Has the committee provided suggestions for dates and sites?
5. Can the site coordinator have his or her recommendations and ideas ready for discussion at the next meeting?
6. Have you established a Reunion Committee Meeting Schedule?
   Is meeting #2 scheduled in three to four weeks?
7. Has everyone made a note to begin searching for classmates? Each committee member should try to locate 10 classmates before the next meeting.
8. Are we having fun yet?

~ ~

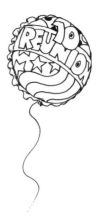

6 - Meeting #2:

~ ~

Goals

- Establish up-front expenses.
- Discuss fundraising requirements.
- Select search leader.
- Select production/mailer committee.
- Set timeline for mailers.

Up-Front Expenses

The unfortunate reality in reunion planning is that the expenses occur before there is cash flow. As you know, there are several steps before classmates start sending in reservation money.

For example, most hotels and museums — the location of your choice — require a non-refundable deposit to reserve the facility. Additionally, there are costs involved in creating the announcement mailer, which consist of the production, printing and postage. On the next page is a list of costs that will be incurred *before* your classmates start sending in checks.

Facility Reservation Deposit

This figure may range from $0 to $2,000 depending on the facility. Don't hesitate to ask the management for a smaller deposit requirement, or better yet, to waive the deposit. Some facilities will take a credit card number and not charge it while you collect money from your classmates. If you are able to negotiate a different deposit set-up, make sure you have it in writing and be certain that your date is confirmed and not jeopardized by this new arrangement.

~ ~

Sample Up-Front Expenses List
Class size: 300

Facility reservation deposit :	$1,000
Mailer: (1X)	
Production cost	200
(.50/person + $50 typeset)	
Postage	150
Envelopes	50
Telephone	200
P.O. Box	100
Labels	20
Ink stamp	25
Total up-front expenses:	$1,745

Printed Materials

Production Cost

The total cost for printed materials should include design, layout and printing charges for the initial mailer. Depending on how resourceful you are, these costs vary. We estimate the average cost of a mailer not to exceed $0.50 per mailing. Add $30 to $50 for the project if you have to hire a professional to to design your mailer.

~ ~

Postage

You will spend $0.50 per mailer on postage, since there will be many returns and re-mailings. The Post Office does offer an address correction service for a fee which varies depending on class of mail, the weight per piece, the accuracy of your list, and the frequency of your mailings. The requirements are quite specific, and can result in a lot of extra expense if done incorrectly — so check, re-check and *re-check* your proposed mailer with the Post Office before you get it printed, to be certain you have everything right.

Bulk mail can save you money, depending on the size of your mailing and the accuracy of your list. Many high school alumni associations have a bulk mail permit which is available for your mailings.

Commercial mailing services can also offer bulk mail rates, as well as valuable information about how to prepare the mailing to save on postage.

Hint

We recommend using the first-class rate unless an alternate method can save you more than 20 percent of your total postage cost.

Envelopes

You will be using a lot of envelopes. Fortunately, standard, white #10 envelopes are not expensive and won't break the bank. Figure $50 for envelopes for a 500 piece mailing.

~ ~

Telephone

Telephone companies love class reunions, because often it takes four to five phone calls to track a missing person. Allot a minimum of $200 for phone calls over a six-month period.

P.O. Box

Your classmates will feel more comfortable sending their checks to a post office box in the name of the reunion, rather than to an individual's home address. Annual fee for a post office box is approximately $100. Open a box in the name of your reunion.

Ink Stamps

Ink stamps are a terrific time saver. Unless you want to handwrite every return address, have a few ink stamps made — for example:

MMHS '85 Reunion
P.O. Box 000
San Diego, CA 92000.

Labels

Mailers always look more professional if they have computer-generated address labels. Storing all the names on a database not only facilitates generating your address labels, but is vital for accounting purposes. Be resourceful! Find that committee member who has a computer. Labels cost approximately $20 per 3,000.

Use your database to determine how much money you will have to raise prior to planning. Keep in mind that you will not have to raise *all* the money for the reunion all at once — just enough funds to cover the start-up expenses. You may find that you can cover all start-up expenses by pre-collecting the committee members' ticket costs. (Or a set amount of, say, $50 per committee member, which will ultimately be deducted from their ticket price for the event.)

The ticket price will vary from city to city, and will depend on how simple or elaborate you want your event to be. The ticket price per person should range from $40 to $65 per person. Discuss, as a committee, the "ideal" ticket price per person. Then, to determine approximate ticket costs, refer to the "Overall Budget Worksheet" at the end of Chapter 7, *Basic Accounting Strategies.*

Remember, these start-up expenses will become part of the overall budget and will be incurred by all classmates.

Well, are you having fun yet?

Fundraising

There are several reasons why your committee may have to consider a fundraiser:

- The class has no reunion fund — needs to cover operating expenses.
- The committee wants to keep ticket price low and defer costs with a fundraiser.

~ ~

- The committee is seeing RED; in other words, you are over budget!
- Committee wants to cover overflow expenses or value-added events such as raffle prizes or drink coupons.

Fundraising: the word itself brings back memories of high school ventures — car washes, The World's Finest Candy Bar sales campaign, and other back-breakers. But before you donate the money needed yourself as an alternative to spending another soapy, sloppy and wet weekend holding yet another carwash, consider fundraising with "adult" methods. Hold a brainstorm session for local alumni. At that meeting, you will come up with ideas for several events.

Actually, a fundraiser is a great way to get classmates excited about the reunion and, at the same time, the occasion lends itself to recruiting additional volunteers for the reunion planning committee. Use every opportunity to "talk up" your class reunion and keep the fires of anticipation and excitement going among your classmates.

Ideas for Pre-Reunion Fundraisers
1. Dinner/Auction. Solicit donations from local businesses and classmates. Gift certificates, sporting tickets, merchandise certificates, a day at the beauty salon, babysitting, dinner coupons, etc. Sell tickets to cover dinner expenses and have an auction or raffle for the donated items. All the proceeds are destined for the class reunion fund.

2. Golf Tournament. This idea was executed successfully by the Class of 1983 from Palm Springs High School. The committee organized a golf tournament at a local public golf course a few months before the reunion. Separate flyers were sent to classmates announcing the event. Event coordinators charged a nominal amount above the standard green fees for tournament prizes and as contributions to the reunion fund. It's another great way to generate reunion excitement and sign up new volunteers for your committee.

3. Picnic and Carnival. Outdoor events are great for attracting families. Hold the picnic at a local park and sell tickets. Hire clowns; organize relay races, face painting and games. Have everyone bring a potluck dish. The ticket price covers a portion of the activity costs and the rest of the proceeds go to the reunion fund. Use it as a testing ground for staging a similar picnic during the reunion weekend. If it works well, do it again.

4. Pancake Breakfast. Pre-sell tickets in your community and to your classmates. Select a weekend morning to host a big pancake breakfast at a local park. The committee and volunteers act as chefs and servers and cheerfully whip up breakfast all morning. Allow enough food for "walk-ups" and try to plan the picnic around an established activity, like a Little League game or soccer tournament. The same formula works well for a spaghetti feast fundraiser as well.

~ ~

5. Solicit business card-size advertisements for the memory book. Classmates can buy a spot to display their business cards in a section of the memory book at a modest rate. For example, if the company who produces your memory book charges you $10 to $20 per page, you can ask for $20 for displaying each business card ad (each memory book page accommodates 8 to 10 business card ads) and make a minimum profit of $180. Announce the information for this advertising opportunity in your mailers and mention it on the reservation form (with a deadline date).

6. Ask for donations in the first mailer. Request donations of services, raffle prizes or cash contributions to the reunion fund. For example, if a classmate happens to have connections to a copy shop, ask for a donation of time or services for producing the mailers. You will be surprised how many of your classmates will gladly contribute to the reunion in the form of a donated service or goods.

Fundraising at the Reunion

It is easy to raise funds at the reunion itself to help cover overflow expenses or have people make donations for the next reunion and the new planning committee. The operative word for planing a fundraiser at the reunion party is *easy,* because at this point you want to be able to enjoy all of your hard work. The following ideas can be pre-planned, executed by the check-in staff and announced by the disc jockey.

Ideas

1. Raffle off centerpieces, class memorabilia, or a vintage year bottle of wine. Sell raffle tickets at check in and during cocktail reception.

2. Here's a 90s idea! Buy some disposable cameras with flash (i.e., Kodak Funsavers®) at bulk price. (Warehouse stores offer them in bulk). Sell your classmates cameras at the check-in. You'll be surprised, these clever little cameras sell like hot cakes. A lot of people don't want to bother traveling with a camera or forget to bring it, but they all want to capture their sentimental time on film.

My classmate Kelly attended the reunion of the class ahead of us. She arrived at the reunion without a camera, not realizing it would be the one thing she really needed. She had a blast reminiscing with schoolmates who actually thought she was in their graduating class. The next time we got together, she told me all about the reunion. Knowing that she rarely goes anywhere without her camera, my first question to her was, "Did you take a picture of so-and-so?" I was surprised to hear that she hadn't even thought of taking a camera to the event. How nice it would have been if she had the opportunity to purchase an inexpensive, disposable

~ ~

camera at check-in and bring her memories home in living color. I would have loved to have seen pictures of how those heartthrobs looked ten years later!

Search Leader

Searching for classmates involves the entire committee. *Everybody* will be involved in this task until the day of the reunion. Put a high priority on the search for classmates! The sooner you begin searching, the better your attendance will be. You are planning a great party for your classmates, but if you don't find them, your efforts are in vain.

Etch the phrase, *"the more the merrier,"* into your mind. Take every opportunity to locate those elusive classmates. You'll find them!

The search leader coordinates all search efforts by organizing committee search meetings, placing announcements in newspapers, updating mailing lists, and monitoring the "missing" list. The search leader works closely with the mailer committee. Ask committee members to submit names with addresses or information on classmates to the search leader as soon as they become available. (See also Chapter 8, *Searching for Classmates.*)

Mailers

Reunion mailers serve several different functions. Your first mailer will initiate the search for fellow classmates.

The size of your class and budget determine how many mailings you will need. A good formula to use is:

Class Size:
- 500 or less = one mailer/with response card + invitation
- 501 or more = mailer/with response card + invitation + "last chance" mailer

In other words, you'll have two mailings for smaller classes and at least three mailings for the larger one. For example, for a larger class, you might send out the first mailer, then the invitation, and, closer to the reunion date, send a followup "last chance." (This is also the "who's coming" letter.) The mailers can be adapted to your needs — just remember your goals:

1. Finding your classmates.
2. Getting commitments ($) to attend.

Mailers should be sent out at three-month intervals. Determine when:

- The initial mailer will be sent.
- If a second mailer is necessary (request payment).
- Invitations with request for payment will be mailed out (4 to 6 months before reunion).
- Follow-up "last chance" letter (one month prior to final head-count deadline).

~ ~

Delegate this task to someone who can produce the mailers and who will oversee the mail-out.

This volunteer works closely with the search leader, who provides the updated mailing lists. Unless this person has a committee, the entire reunion committee should be aware of the mailer timeline and be prepared to assist in the task of getting the mailing ready. (See also Chapter 8, *Searching For Classmates.*)

Meeting #2 in Review

1. What are your anticipated up-front expenses?
2. How will the up-front expenses be funded?
3. Will you have to do a fundraiser?
   If yes, who will organize the fundraiser?
   What kind of a fundraiser will it be ?
   When and where will it take place?
4. Who is your search leader?
5. Are committee members submitting information on classmates to the search leader?
6. Who will be in charge of producing the mailers?
7. Who will organize the initial mailing?
8. What is the timeline for mailers to be sent out?
9. When is your next committee meeting?

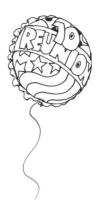

7 - Basic Accounting Strategies

~ ~

Selecting a Money Manager

Money will be coming in, and money will be going out! Remember the basic principle of good economics: the former should be a larger figure than the latter!

We are not here to teach you how to balance a budget, but we offer some suggestions on how to make reunion money management easier and worry-free. First of all, if there is a committee member with accounting or book-keeping skills, tap that resource. Whether you keep the books yourself or have someone help you, adopt the

~ ~

following simple steps that will help keep handling of the money manageable.

Open a reunion checking and/or savings account. This enables your classmates to write checks to the *Reunion Fund* instead of making out a check to an individual. Most importantly, a checking account is a legal record of all transactions, and every penny of income is easily traceable. More than one person should be authorized to sign on the account, in case one or the other is unavailable when bills have to be paid, or deposits are to be made.

Note

Should you open an interest-bearing account using your Social Security number, you will have to pay taxes on the interest. You may want to consider a non-interest bearing checking account. In that case, the reunion committee must apply for a checking account under "unincorporated group" status. The bank will require that the group assume a formal name.

1. Form a "group," such as *MMHS Reunion Planning Group.*

2. Appoint officers; designate a president, vice president, secretary and treasurer. Record the designation of officers in the minutes from the meeting and all officers must sign the minutes — thus becoming authorized signers on the account.

~ ~

3. Get a tax identification number. One of the officers' Social Security numbers would suffice.

All of the above three items are required to open a non-interest bearing account. The alternative is to form a non-profit group, which is a complicated and involved process that requires forming a corporation with bylaws and elected officers, acquiring an advisory board, applying to the IRS for non-profit status, and tax identification.

Now, forming an unincorporated group sounds simple, doesn't it?

Hint

Keep a simple ledger in which you enter each payment, list the name (using last name used in high school), of sender, the amount and date of payment (see Sample Spreadsheet on next page). This ledger acts as a backup to your R.S.V.P. list. Make a xerox copy of every check or money order you receive before depositing it. File the copies for easy reference, in case a question about payment arises.

Keep a close eye on the budget and report all money activities regularly to your committee. Give each committee member a copy of the established budget so that everyone is well informed as to what is needed — when and how much. Notify your committee in advance in case you are not meeting your projections, so you can get your heads together and make plans for a fundraiser. (See Chapter 6, *Meeting #2,* "Fundraising" Section.)

~ ~

SAMPLE SPREADSHEET – TRACKING RESERVATIONS

LAST NAME	FIRST NAME	MARRIED NAME	RSVP #	DATE REC'D	AMT. REC'D	BAL. DUE	OTHER	SPOUSE/ GUEST
Rowe	Janet		1	4/26/94	$55	$0	Q	N/A
Raite	Sally	Little	2	3/14/94	$110	$0		Tom Little
Trent	Adam		0		$20	$0	MB	
Ward	Bill		2	4/18/94	$110	$0	Q	Linda Ward

~ ~

It is extremely important for you to develop a system to track your reservations. The information you will need includes:

- Name (last name used in high school, first name, married name).
- Number attending.
- Confirmation of payment.
- Guest/spouse name.
- Memory book order.
- Questionnaire received.

You will be able to use this list for a final head count when ordering your memory books and to create name tags. You will also use this information as your RSVP or "pre-paid checklist" at the check-in tables.

The sample on the previous page includes some of the required information. Maintain notations for new last names using parentheses or "other" category. Always sort by last name used in school to be consistent and refer to last names used in school to cross-check your original class list for unaccounted people. Use symbols to identify categories like:

Q = Questionnaire received, or

MB = Memory Book ordered. (Since classmates who are attending receive a memory book as part of the ticket price, an MB designation would indicate that the person is not attending, but wishes to purchase a memory book. See "Trent, Adam" on sample spreadsheet on previous page.)

~ ~

Creating the Overall Budget

The money manager has the not-so-coveted task of creating the overall budget. However daunting the task may seem, we are here to make it easier. There are three phases to creating the budget: information gathering, committee review and finalizing.

Phase One: Information Gathering

You will rely on your committee members to supply you with preliminary budget requests. One way to expedite the process is to give each sub-committee leader a worksheet with his or her budget categories highlighted (see page 74). Ask them to investigate their budget needs and get back to you with a realistic and reasonable figure by a specific date. For example, ask the site coordinator to provide you with costs for the facility/room, food, A/V rental, linens, set-up, etc. by next meeting. This will require the subcommittee to evaluate what they will need to complete their task.

Each cost should be itemized so the committee can review each expenditure separately. For example, if the decorations committee includes floral arrangements with personalized wine centerpieces, both the cost for the flowers and the wine should be outlined. On the worksheet, the cost will appear as one figure, but the committee may consider floral arrangements too expensive and request a different proposal from the decorations committee before they approve it. We recommend that, as the reunion committee leader, you also do your own research with regards to the entire budget so you will have a comparison figure.

~ ~

Phase Two: Committee Review

Present the individual budget requests to the reunion committee as a whole at the next scheduled meeting. Using the budget worksheet, create a preliminary budget using the "ideal" budgets submitted by the sub-committees. Then, use the ticket price formula to ballpark the cost per person (see "Sample Overall Budget" at the end of this chapter). If your ticket price is reasonable, you will have to make very few changes. If not, there may be lengthy committee discussion.

It is important to make the information clear and the presentation smooth. This procedure may take the majority of a meeting, so allot time for it. Impartially present the budget requests, summarize the requested items and initiate a brief discussion. Make changes as necessary. The committee may request that the subcommittee gather more information. Offer any comparison figures you may have obtained.

Hint

Discuss your committee's goals for ticket price so you know ahead of time approximately how much you will need to cut from the budget requests. Keep a running tally of "dollars added or cut" as you make changes.

Even if you reach your goal before you have presented all the budget requests, go through all of them. You may find more items to cut and salvage those wine centerpieces that lost by a narrow margin.

~ ~

Phase Three: Finalizing the Budget

Whew! Budget meetings are seldom fun, but we hope your discussions went smoothly. Now, with all the changes and additional information you've gathered, it's time to finalize the budget. As the money manager, you have final say with regards to the budget. After your strenuous meeting, hopefully you will simply just "fill in the blanks" of the worksheet. Compile all the figures approved at the meeting to complete the budget. Provide copies of the final budget to all committee members and remind them that you have an aversion to the color red!

Managing the Overall Budget

Like an ebb and flow, thus will be your money supply. Committees will be spending money and classmates will be sending in their reservation payments. We've discussed how to track reservations, and now we offer several hints about how to track accounts payable.

~ ~

Hints

1. Ask your committee members to submit check requests in writing using a similar format:

Requestor: Date:
Committee:
Check Amount: For:
Made Payable To:
Send To (name, address):
(Attach invoice or receipt.)

---

2. Maintain a log for each budget category to gauge the balance available. Fill in the actual costs as the figures become available.

3. Create accountability by asking each subcommittee leader to know where they stand with regards to their budget. Verify their information with your running tally. Do not make it a full-time job.

~ ~

Sample Overall Budget Worksheet
Based on class size of 500 = 175 attendance

	Budget	Actual Cost
Up-front expenses:		
Site deposit	$ 500	_____
Initial mailer production,		
$.50/person + $50	300	_____
Postage, $.50/person	250	_____
Phone	350	_____
P.O. Box	100	_____
Supplies (labels, ink stamp, envelopes)	100	_____
Subtotal:	$1,600	_____
Mailers (each):		
Production, $.50/person + $50	300	_____
Postage, $.40/person	200	_____
Subtotal:	$ 500	_____
Site/Facility:		
Room charge (if applicable)	N/A	_____
Food cost ($25/person)	4,375	_____
Audio/Visual equipment rental		
(if applicable)	200	_____
Rentals (linen, tables, decorations)		
(if applicable)	N/A	_____
Subtotal:	$4,575	_____
less site deposit	(500)	_____
	$4,075	_____

~ ~

Sample Overall Budget Worksheet (cont'd.)

	Budget	Actual Cost
Event:		
Decorations ($1/person)	175	_____
Program ($1/person)	175	_____
Music ($4/person)	700	_____
Photographer	0	_____
Awards/Gifts ($.75/person)	131	_____
Photo name badges ($2/person)	350	_____
Slide show/Video ($2/person)	350	_____
Subtotal:	$ 1,881	_____
Miscellaneous:		
Memory book ($10/person)	1,750	_____
Faculty guests (2)	120	_____
Weekend event fund ($1/person)	175	_____
Reserve fund($1/person)	175	_____
Subtotal:	2,210	_____
Total budget:	$10,276	
Actual cost:		_____

Ticket price formula:
Total budget/Estimated attendance = Ticket price per person

$10,276/175 = $58.72 per person

~ ~

Overall Budget Worksheet

Based on class size of ___ = ___ attendance

	Budget	Actual Cost
Up-front expenses:		
Site deposit	_____	_____
Initial mailer production	_____	_____
Postage	_____	_____
Phone	_____	_____
P.O. Box	_____	_____
Supplies (labels, ink stamp, etc.)	_____	_____
Subtotal:	_____	_____
Mailers (each):		
Production	_____	_____
Postage	_____	_____
Subtotal:	_____	_____
Site/Facility		
Room charge (if applicable)	_____	_____
Food cost	_____	_____
Audio/Visual equipment rental (if applicable)	_____	_____
Rentals (linen, tables, decorations) (if applicable)	_____	_____
_____	_____	_____
Subtotal:(less site deposit)	_____	_____

~ ~

Overall Budget Worksheet (cont'd.)

	Budget	Actual Cost
Event:		
Decorations	_____	_____
Program	_____	_____
Music	_____	_____
Photographer	_____	_____
Awards/Gifts	_____	_____
Name badges	_____	_____
Slide show	_____	_____
Subtotal:	_____	_____
Miscellaneous:		
Memory book	_____	_____
Faculty guests	_____	_____
Weekend event fund	_____	_____
Reserve fund	_____	_____
Subtotal:	_____	_____
Total budget:	_____	
Actual cost:		_____

Ticket price formula:

Total budget/Estimated attendance = Ticket price per person

8 - Searching for Classmates

~ ~

What are the fondest memories that people take with them from their reunion? It's certainly not the food or the music, no matter how great both turned out. What people will remember the most is *reuniting* with their high school buddies they haven't seen for years — old friends they lost touch with, former "flames" and rivals. People look forward with great anticipation to reminiscing about the long-ago yesterdays, and to chatting up a storm with a favorite — or not so favorite — teacher. And, finally, they will be able to satisfy their curiosity about whatever happened to so-and-so.

~ ~

A reunion is about people — classmates — that's what they came for and that's who they expect to find at the reunion. For that reason alone, the search leader's top priority is to round up all those so-and-sos and, if possible, more so-and-sos.

Basically, all your other efforts for producing a terrific event are for naught if you don't have a good turnout. To achieve that, you must use effective searching techniques and allow yourselves enough time to locate your classmates and teachers. Go through your yearbooks to jog your memory. Start your own investigating program and as you collect fresh information about the whereabouts of classmates, provide the committee with updated lists. You will be amazed how many people you will find when you start the ball rolling.

When I started planning my own high school reunion and subsequently began searching for classmates, I was seeing classmates everywhere. I was convinced that a fellow walking out of a deli was one of our popular football players.

This was becoming an obsession with me because I wanted to make sure we found them all. The irony about these incidents was the fact that I lived 1,200 miles away from where I went to school. It was absurd and more than unlikely to run into anyone from home base. I finally decided that my "seeing" classmates at every step was simply the result of poring over the yearbook and making phone calls to locate elusive classmates. A friendly suggestion to you as you embark on the "search" is to keep the

~ ~

task in the back of your mind — you might just find one when you're not even looking.

Hint

When delegating search tasks always set *due dates* for their completion. Everything about the search for classmates takes time. Hold committee members responsible for finding a certain number of classmates and impress on them that this needs to be done in as timely a manner as possible.

As we mentioned before, the search is a constant, almost never-ending process and involves everyone on the committee. The following search methods should be put into action simultaneously rather than chronologically.

1. Place a Public Service Announcement (PSA) in your local newspaper. (See Chapter 3, *Background on Reunions*, "Startup Chores" Section.)

2. Initial mailer. If this is the first class reunion you are planning since graduation, rely on the class list provided by your high school. If this list is not available, refer to Chapter 8, *Searching for Classmates*, "Starting from Scratch/No Class List Available" Section. The addresses you are obtaining from your high school are primarily your classmates' parents' addresses. Ask committee members to contact the classmates they know and obtain updated addresses, phone numbers and note changes of names.

~ ~

Request address corrections from the Post Office. (For more information, see Chapter 6, *Meeting #2*, "Printed Materials" Section, "Postage" Subsection.) Send the re-addressed mailer out again at once to the new address to confirm the accuracy of the information.

From the results of the initial mailer, you will learn who is missing. Mailers that are returned stamped *undeliverable* immediately become "missing classmates." Compile a "missing" list.

3. Tracking through "current occupant." If your initial mailer is returned with the stamped notice: *Forwarding Order Expired*, try to track your classmate through the current residents of that address. Write a letter to that person explaining your purpose in contacting the former occupant and address the letter to "Current Occupant." (If the address turns out to be an apartment building, you may have better luck contacting the apartment manager.) In your letter, ask the resident to assist you in finding your classmate's new address. If the new occupant doesn't know it, a neighbor might be able to help. Most importantly, enclose a self-addressed, stamped envelope for convenience — it will increase the response rate.

4. Phone book party. The next step is for the search leader to organize a phone book party. Each committee member arrives armed with a variety of telephone books and the class' high school year book. With the

~ ~

"missing" list in hand and lots of pizza and refreshments, the reunion committee looks through the yearbook and local phone books in their search for locating classmates and to ferret out parents' phone numbers. These parties are not only a lot of fun, but they are extremely effective in locating those "missing" classmates, since approximately 50 percent of parents are still in the area. As the phone numbers become available, several people should be placing calls to locate the missing persons. These calls generate excitement among the committee members as well as the classmates you contact.

For the more sophisticated groups, the White Pages are available in most cities on CD-ROM. Check your local phone company for availability, cost and software requirements.

5. Second mailer or invitation with "missing" list included. This mailer repeats the information provided in the initial mailer and offers further details of the reunion. An important part of this mailer is the enclosed "missing" list. Include a list of "missing" classmates in the mailer and encourage people to call in the information they have on these classmates.

6. Radio PSAs. Local radio stations have public service announcements slots available. Provide the radio station with a press release indicating who, what, where, when, and include a contact person's name and telephone number.

~ ~

7. Alumni. Check the local college alumni directories for names and addresses. Most university alumni associations have directories available. Call the association directly. If your high school has an alumni group, it will be beneficial, because members may be identified by the last name they used in high school.

8. High school. Don't neglect the obvious. Your high school can be your greatest source of information beyond the act of providing the class list. Some high schools have alumni groups who will help you find members from your graduating class. The school is also the best place to look for former teachers. If the teacher is still teaching in the district, the high school can locate him or her through the system. And finally, ask the high school to announce the date of your reunion on the school's marquee. Include a contact person's phone number on the marquee.

9. Social Security letter forwarding. For the die-hard searchers, contacting the Social Security Administration Letter Forwarding Unit takes time and know-how, but the results can be satisfying. Here is how it works:

   First, write a letter to your missing classmate and place it in an unsealed, stamped envelope. Forward the letter to the Social Security Administration with a cover letter explaining why you are searching for this person. Ideally, provide all the information you have on the missing person: full name, birth date, place of birth, last known address, or Social Security number (some of the

~ ~

information may be on your class list). The Social Security Administration will send your letter to your classmate if he is registered with the administration. Send correspondence to:

Social Security Administration
c/o Letter Forwarding Unit
6401 Security Boulevard
Baltimore, Maryland, 21235

10. Database. We recommend the following method for locating a missing classmate as a last resort. There are database companies which can search for missing classmates. Most companies charge a fee per name, have minimum requirements, and do not guarantee that the person they locate is the person you are looking for. However, by the time you get to this point, you've tried all the other ways to find your classmate. If you have no clues, and you want to continue the search, a database company is one more possibility to aid you in your effort.

~ ~

Starting from Scratch/ No Class List Available

Beginning the search process from scratch can be a daunting task, but amazingly enough, most reunion committees start with nothing but a yearbook and determination. Before the age of information stored on computer disks, one copy of the class list was usually saved somewhere. This casual method provided unlimited opportunities for a list to disappear forever. If your committee cannot locate a copy of your class list, use the following guidelines to get your search underway.

1. Organize a phone book party right away. Gather your committee armed with phone books and yearbooks. Start looking up classmates names in the phone books. In many cases, you will find their parents' name and phone number. This is the best place to start. Call the parents and ask them for their son's or daughter's phone number and/or address. Always introduce yourself and explain your purpose for obtaining the information. The classmates who cannot be located are placed on the "missing" list.

   The phone book party(ies) are bound to start a chain reaction.

2. Every time you get a classmate on the phone, ask him for names and addresses of someone with whom your party stayed in touch. Leave him your telephone

~ ~

number or that of the search leader's in case he will be able to provide additional information at a later time.

3. Whenever you gather new information on a classmate, another door opens. If you discover that Mary Rodgers' married name is Mary Levin, look up her "new" name in the phone book. That may be all it takes to find Mary Rodgers.

4. Ask the search leader to provide the committee with updated copies of the "missing" list. You could hit a bonanza if you run into a long lost friend at the mall and she can give you information on several "missing" classmates.

5. Incorporate the strategies and methods listed in the first part of this chapter.

Faculty Guests

My high school principal was great. He roamed the campus and made friends with most of the students. He was on the scene all year 'round. We were quite fond of him, called him "Mr. V" and were sincere when we laughed at all his jokes. It would be great to see him at our 10-year reunion. He'd probably still try to stump us with his-spoon-on-the-nose trick.

Everyone has a favorite faculty member from high school. It is a wonderful surprise to discover favorite teachers as guests at the reunion. Just as we are curious to

~ ~

discover what happened to our contemporaries, faculty members are equally interested in how their students turned out. It makes for a real get-together.

Among your committee, develop a diversified list of potential faculty members you'd like to invite to the next reunion. Be certain to add the question, "Who was your favorite teacher?" to your questionnaire. Include these faculty members on your search list — several of them may no longer be at your old school. Use the high school as a resource to find these people — faculty members can often be tracked down through the school district.

Depending on how many faculty members you select to invite, you may consider inviting them as guests or reduce the ticket price for them. Some committees add a nominal amount to the ticket price — usually $1 to $2 — in order to cover the costs for faculty guests. If, for instance, you have sold 200 tickets, you will have enough money to invite four to five faculty guests.

There is also the option to defer part of the ticket price for invited guests. Some committees charge faculty members for the dinner and the Memory Book only. Create special invitations for your faculty guests if you are waiving or reducing the price.

My class had a lengthy and varied list for faculty guests. We chose to invite our class advisor and principal as our guests — free of charge — while other faculty members were invited at a reduced cost. With little effort, yet an impressive presentation, we sent personalized invitations to all faculty guests. Our secret was to use a "create your own card" machine. We used Hallmark™ because of the

~ ~

stationery selection, but many drug stores and card shops are introducing this way to customize invitations.

Hint

For approximately the cost of a birthday card, customize your faculty invitations on a "create your own card" machine at your local card shop.

If you simply cannot afford to have non-paying guests, don't abandon the idea of inviting them to the festivities. Send them the same invitations the classmates receive. There always will be several faculty members who will choose to attend regardless of the fact that they have to pay their own way. They understand. Have photo badges made for them — it will make them feel part of the reunion.

~ ~

Complimentary Faculty Invitation

MMHS Class of 1985 invites you to be our special guest at our

10 year Reunion Party on
Saturday, May 13, 1995 at the
U.S. Grant Hotel, San Diego.
Festivities begin at 6:00 p.m.
Dinner at 7:00 p.m.
Please R.S.V.P. by using the
enclosed form. See you soon!

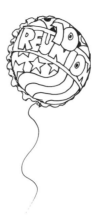

9 - Database Strategies

~ ~

Encourage your search leader to build a master database of all your classmates, using your class list from the school. Update the master list constantly with the new information, as addresses, phone numbers and change of names become available. There are several ways to accomplish this task. With all the advanced computer science at our disposal, it may seem antiquated to use an old fashioned ledger for record keeping. However, if you prefer taking pencil to pad you can still adapt the computer system to meet your needs.

~ ~

On a basic spreadsheet program, you can monitor a variety of information about your classmates. Set up the database with the following information:

- Name (sort alphabetically — by last names used in high school).
- Address.
- Phone.
- Date of last update.
- Comments. For example, you may have a classmate named Jackie Brenner who is married to Frank Stewart, is donating a gift certificate to the raffle and has just recently been "found." See what her record would look like on the next page.

The category "Updated" is important so you can monitor how recently you recorded the information. For example, the record for David Callison shows "1985" in the updated column. This means that the information provided is from the original class list and hasn't been updated yet. Periodically, you can sort by "1985" to add/delete names from the "missing" list.

With a spreadsheet program, you can easily create new categories and add things like "Questionnaire" which would monitor whether a questionnaire has been received or "R.S.V.P.," to indicate how many will be attending. Modify your database to suit your needs. Ideally, utilize a software program that enables you to extract name, address, city, state, zip code to create mailing labels. Your local computer store or office supply outlet can direct you to the best software program for the job you need to accomplish.

SAMPLE SPREADSHEET - MASTER LIST

LAST NAME	FIRST NAME	TITLE	MARRIED NAME	ADDRESS	CITY/ST/ZIP	PHONE	UPDATED	COMMENTS
Brenner	Jackie	Mrs	Stewart	111 Dayton Pl	Bothell, WA 98011	123-555-0000	5/27/94	Donate gift cert.
Callison	David	Mr.		3500 Meridien St	Redlands CA 92006	321-555-9999	1985	parents address

~ ~

Remember, your database information must remain strictly confidential. You will have a wealth of information about your classmates at your fingertips and it is important that your committee uses the information discreetly. It is an unfortunate reality that we must warn you of the possibility the information could be abused. Your committee may get phone calls from classmates or other persons asking questions about their "long lost friend." It is imperative that you have your classmates' permission to release information about them before you comply with a request.

10 – Producing Effective Mailers

Initial Mailers

Since you've already established your timeline for mailers, give yourself enough time to create them. The purpose of the initial mailer is to generate response for updating names and addresses. Therefore, the mailer needs to be concise, informative and prepared for a quick and easy way for returning. Remember, this is your first communication with many of your classmates since graduation, so convey your excitement about the upcoming event as a committee. Let them know just what they have to look forward to and how everyone is chomping at the bit to get there! If you can convince your classmates that the reunion will be *fun*, they won't think twice about attending or responding to your mailer. Following is a sample of an initial mailer designed to be reversible for easy return.

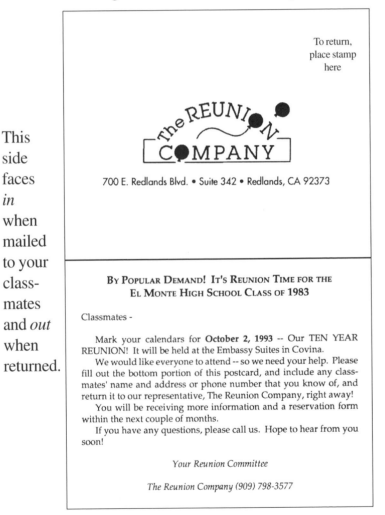

To return,
place stamp
here

This side faces *in* when mailed to your classmates and *out* when returned.

THE REUNION COMPANY

700 E. Redlands Blvd. • Suite 342 • Redlands, CA 92373

By POPULAR DEMAND! IT'S REUNION TIME FOR THE
EL MONTE HIGH SCHOOL CLASS OF 1983

Classmates -

Mark your calendars for **October 2, 1993** -- Our TEN YEAR REUNION! It will be held at the Embassy Suites in Covina.

We would like everyone to attend -- so we need your help. Please fill out the bottom portion of this postcard, and include any classmates' name and address or phone number that you know of, and return it to our representative, The Reunion Company, right away!

You will be receiving more information and a reservation form within the next couple of months.

If you have any questions, please call us. Hope to hear from you soon!

Your Reunion Committee

The Reunion Company (909) 798-3577

~ ~

The REUNION COMPANY

700 E. Redlands Blvd.
Suite 342
Redlands, CA 92373

This side faces *out* when mailed to your classmates, and *in* when returned.

Mailing label
to classmates

EL MONTE CLASS OF 1983

Your Name: _____
ladies include maiden name

Address: _____

_____

Phone: (_____) _____

Please list the names and addresses (or phone numbers) of all classmates you know the whereabouts of:

_____
_____
_____
_____

This Postcard Has Distinct Characteristics

1. The mailer can be a postcard, thereby saving on postage.

2. When it is folded inside-out, it is self-addressed for easy return.
3. It introduces the event and established details, like date and location.
4. It provides a phone number for people who'd rather call in their information.
5. The instructions are clear and direct.
6. It conveys *fun!*
7. Use a colored paper that represents your high school colors announcing "REUNION" or "CLASS OF 19XX" in bold lettering on the front of the card. Your mailer will stand out and attract the attention of your classmates.
8. Incorporate good graphics, logos or slogans, like "CLASS OF '88 STILL GREAT!" in all your mailers to make all reunion correspondence immediately identifiable.

If card stock is available in your school colors — by all means, use it! The initial mailer is the first thing that spells R-e-u-n-i-o-n to your classmates, and first impressions are important. Whether or not you have the budget for fancy paper, printing or graphics, the best thing in any case is to keep it simple. People identify with simplicity. It is also important that your message doesn't get lost in a heap of fluff.

Keep your mailers simple, utilizing school colors, logos and appealing, fun phrases, and you'll be sure to increase the response rate.

~ ~

Search Mailers

If you have a large class and are sending two letters, your initial mailer may not have offered many details about the reunion. Your second mailer, however, should elaborate on the activities of the event. By now, you know where and when the reunion will take place — so inform everyone in detail. Make your message exciting and inviting. Provide as much event information as possible so your classmates will not be able to refuse the invitation.

We have also discovered that by using the standard $8^{1}/_{2}$ X 11 format for paper, you will reach more people. The paper can be fancy and the graphics creative, but keep your message on one sheet of paper. I have seen reunion materials that look like wedding invitations — half a dozen pieces that fall out of the envelope. These odd pieces either don't get read, are misplaced or get lost. (They are costly, too.)

The second mailer should include, on a separate sheet, a list of "missing persons" — all the ones for whom you have no addresses. Encourage your classmates to review the list and supply information on the missing classmates. On this mailer, include information on the cost for sleeping rooms, meals, etc. and provide a reservation form for easy return.

The format for this mailer should follow the same guidelines as the first mailer. Be concise and clear with your message and the layout, but keep the tone upbeat and the prognosis *fun*. Because there is a lot of information to convey, categorize it item by item. (See sample on next page.)

~ ~

Sample Search Mailer
Front - Detailed Event Information
Back (not shown) - "Missing" List

Mira Mesa High School
Class of 1985
Ten Year Reunion
"Class of '85
Still Alive in '95"

Saturday, May 13, 1995
U.S. Grant Hotel
326 Broadway
San Diego, California

6:00 p.m. Reception / No-Host Bar
7:30 p.m. Dinner / Dance
Dress: Semi-Formal

Update
Reservation Deadline

The deadline is approaching quickly. Please return full payment of $60.00 by April 1, 1995. We want everybody there. So call all of your MMHS friends and give them that encouraging nudge to join in on the fun.

An Added Extra

The first 30 people who send in their reservation form and check by March 1, 1995 will be entered in a drawing for a free room at U.S. Grant Hotel the night of the Reunion. For those of you who have already sent your reservation form and check, you will also be entered in the drawing.

Friday Night

May 12th - 7:00 p.m.
Cocktail Party - (Drinks on your own)
U.S. Grant Lobby Bar

Family Picnic

Sunday, May 14th - 11:00 a.m.
Mariners Point - Across from the Roller Coaster
B.Y.O.E. - Bring your own everything

HOTEL ACCOMMODATIONS: A limited number of rooms are being blocked in the name of your school. Make room reservations directly to the U.S. Grant Hotel - 1-800-334-6957. Be sure to specify you are with Mira Mesa '85 to receive a discounted room rate. ROOMS ARE LIMITED.

MEMORY BOOK: If you are unable to attend your reunion, you can still experience the excitement of seeing your old classmates! Mail a photo of yourself and your family and $20.00 to The Reunion Company and you will receive a memory book that includes candid photos of the evening's festivities, a class directory, and current photos of your classmates! Don't Miss Out!

MISSING LIST: Please check the missing list for the people we could not locate. If you know where to find anyone listed, please send that information along with your questionnaire and check or call The Reunion Company at (909) 798-3577 or 1-800-315-3577.

Your Reunion Committee

Mike DeRisi	Lorie McKee	Holly Santiago
Tamara Kalke	Kim McElliott Foster	Tammy McDaniel Gray
Sharon Ramat	Kim Walther	Joel Diaz
Kirk Van Wagoner	Connie Vlado	Kelly Rudiger

For Additional Information: The Reunion Co. is working with your reunion committee in the planning of this reunion. If you have any questions, please call (909) 798-3577 or 1-800-315-3577. Our address is 700 E. Redlands Blvd., #342, Redlands, CA 92373. **Please contact us if you did not receive the first invitation/reservation form.**

~ ~

Include the following information:

1. Who, what, where, when, and how much.
   Describe the memory book and its cost and availability to classmates who are unable to attend.

2. Solicit business card advertisements (optional fundraiser).

3. "Missing" persons list.

4. Reservation form
   Offer a prepaid ticket price and walk-up ticket price.

5. Will there be a limited number of walk-up spaces available? If so, let your classmates know. You want people to make reservations ahead of time.
   - Describe the cancellation policy, i.e., full refund 30 days out, 50 percent refund up to two weeks before event, no refunds within two weeks of the event.
   - Note: If the facility for the event requires a final head count more than two weeks ahead of time, adjust your cancellation policy. You do not want to refund money if you have already committed the funds to the caterer.
   - Payment option: We suggest you accept checks or money orders only. Remind classmates to make checks payable to the reunion fund (Example: BHS Reunion).
   - The search goes on. Designate space on the reservation form for information on classmates.

~ ~

6. Questionnaire. The questionnaire provides the information to be used in the memory book and/or awards ceremony. Special prizes may be awarded for the most unusual answers. Request basic information:

- Full name.
- Last name used in high school,
- Address.
- Phone (not distributed).
- Occupation.
- Marital status.
- Wedding date.
- Spouse/guest's name, children's names and ages.

But also include creative questions that lend themselves well to special awards, like:

- When I graduated I wanted to be (occupation), and now I am …
- My most memorable moments of my high school days were …
- In high school, I wanted to date …
- The song that most reminds me of the good old days is …

The information you plan to use in your program for that special evening should be mentioned in this questionnaire. (See sample on next page.)

7. Additional Information.

- Quote group room rates at the hotel (or a local hotel if event is elsewhere) and how to reserve accommodations. Usually, there is a specific number of

~ ~

MIRA MESA HIGH SCHOOL CLASS OF 1985
10 YEAR REUNION QUESTIONNAIRE

The following information, except the phone number, may be used in our Memory Book, as well as for awards.
Please fill out the form and return it whether you can attend the reunion or not.

Name: _____Maiden Name: _____

Address: (Home) _____

Present Occupation: _____

Home Phone: _____Work Phone: _____

❑ Single ❑ Married _____# Years Married   Name of Spouse or Guest: _____

Spouse's Occupation: _____

List Names and Ages of Children: _____

Are you expecting? _____When is your due date? _____

List 3 Favorite Songs from HS: _____

What was your best memory of HS? _____

Favorite Class Subject: _____

Favorite Teacher: _____

Who did you have a crush on in HS? _____

What was your most embarrassing moment in HS? _____

Who did you vote for in '92 for President? _____

Where is your favorite vacation spot? _____

What are your hobbies or interests? _____

Did anyone marry his/her high school sweetheart? _____Who? _____

Did he/she graduate from the Class of '85? _____What Class? _____

When I graduated from HS, I wanted to be _____(occupation)

Now I'm _____(occupation)

What song makes you think of "Good Ol' Days?" _____

Who do you hope to see at the reunion? _____

Who did you want to date in HS? _____

What is something you wanted to do in HS but never did? _____

We are putting together a photo collage for the night of the reunion. If you'd like to participate, please send us
any photos, past or present. Be sure to include your name (maiden name) on the back of the photos and send
them to:

The Reunion Company
700 E. Redlands Blvd., Ste 342
Redlands, CA 92373
1 (800) 315-3577
FAX (909) 792-7994

• Photos will not be returned •

Please send or FAX survey by May 1, 1995 to the Above Address

~ ~

rooms in the reserved block. Convey to your classmates that the group-rate rooms are first-come, first-served. If there is a deadline for honoring the discounted rate, include that information as well.

• Ask classmates who cannot attend to submit a photo of themselves and/or their family to be included in the memory book section, "Classmates We Missed." Advise them that the photos cannot be returned.

• Include information on additional activities for the weekend — the golf tournament, picnic or cocktail party.

The Invitation

This is the formal invitation to the event. Provide a condensed version of the information included in the search mailer (see page 97). The format for the invitation is up to you. Some classes simply send a mailer similar to their earlier ones, others create a different and more formal invitation to send. The style and quality of your final invitation depends largely on your budget. At this point, you will have a fairly accurate mailing list, so expect to reach a higher percentage of your classmates with this mailer than ever before.

If you can afford to jazz up the invitation, by all means, do it. Every piece of communication reflects what your classmates can expect from the reunion party. If this is your final mailing, indicate that this is the "last chance" reminder for the reunion. (See sample on next four pages.)

~ ~

You may want to send the formal invitation after the initial mailer. Depending on your timeline and progress in locating people, the search mailer or a "last chance" mailer may follow the invitation.

Front of Sample Invitation

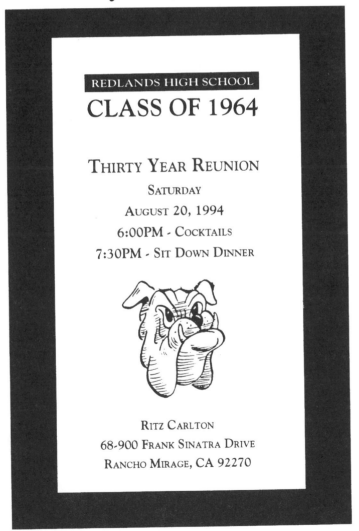

REDLANDS HIGH SCHOOL

CLASS OF 1964

THIRTY YEAR REUNION

SATURDAY
AUGUST 20, 1994
6:00PM - COCKTAILS
7:30PM - SIT DOWN DINNER

RITZ CARLTON
68-900 FRANK SINATRA DRIVE
RANCHO MIRAGE, CA 92270

~ ~

Sample Invitation, Inside

REUNION PACKAGES

REUNION EVENING

Sit Down Dinner (No Host Bar)
Entertainment - Music by The Tornadoes
Photo Name Badges
Door Prizes
Memory Book
Many More Surprises

$60.00 per person (Pre-Pay)
$70.00 per person at the door - Cash Only

———————————— ❧ ————————————

If you are unable to attend the reunion, you still may purchase a Memory Book.
It will contain portraits of each classmate in attendance, candid photos from the
evening, a directory of all classmates returning questionnaires, and a "classmates
we missed" section with photos of people who couldn't come to the reunion. If
you cannot attend, please send in a recent photo of yourself (or you and your
family) so you can still be included in the Memory Book. All books will be
mailed approximately 4 months after the reunion.

Memory Books are $20.00 each

———————————— ❧ ————————————

If you want to make the most of your weekend, make plans to stay at the Ritz
Carlton. Special room rates will be given if you mention you're with the RHS
'64 Reunion. Contact the hotel directly:

(619) 321-8282 or 800-241-3333
68-900 Frank Sinatra Drive
Rancho Mirage, CA 92270

$70.00 per night

~ ~

Sample Invitation, Inside

QUESTIONNAIRE

Please fill out and return questionnaire whether you plan
to attend the reunion or not.

Name: _____ Maiden Name: _____

Address: _____

Phone: (H) _____   Occupation: _____
       (W) _____

Spouse's/Guest's Name: _____

No. of children: _____ names and ages: _____

Grandchildren: _____ names and ages: _____

Missing Classmates: _____

If you would like to donate a prize for the raffle and/or advertise in our
Memory Book, please contact Mary Jo Guia Holmes (909) 793-4798.

RESERVATION FORM

Tickets will be held at the door

❑ Yes, I'll be there! Please reserve _____ tickets for me. $_____
                                                     amount enclosed

Make checks payable to:
The Reunion Company • 700 E. Redlands Blvd., Ste. 342 • Redlands, CA 92373

Mastercard/VISA also accepted

     ❑ VISA
Card # ❑ M/C _____   Expiration Date   _____

❑ Sorry, I'm going to miss a great time but I would still like to order $ 20.00
a Memory Book. Please include me in the "classmates we missed" section.
I have enclosed a photo for you to include in the Memory Book.

Refund policy: Full refund 30 days prior to the event,
50% refund if cancelled 29 days or less prior to the event.

~ ~

Sample Invitation, Back

Dear Classmates,

This is the Reunion we've all been waiting for -30 years!
Because it will be such a memorable event, we want to
make sure everyone is there. So call all of your RHS
friends and give them that encouraging nudge to join in
the fun and reminiscing. Don't miss out!

See you in August!

Sincerely,
Your Reunion Committee

———

A golf tournament is being planned.
If interested please contact Hank Mercado
(H) 123-555-5555 or (W) 123-555-5432

~ ~

"Last Chance" Mailers

Again, depending on your budget, timing and response rates, you may want to send out a final mailer.

The purpose:

1. Encourage those classmates who haven't responded yet to attend (and send in their reservation).
2. Communicate additional activity information like:
   * Information on Friday night cocktail party "ice-breaker."
   * Golf (or sport) tournament.
   * Sunday picnic.
3. Enclose another questionnaire for those who "misplaced" the first one. Remind them to send it in ahead of time.

A light-hearted approach works well for the "last chance" mailer. Tease your audience with questions like:

* Who traveled the farthest to see *you?*
* Find out who has the most kids.
* Do you remember what you put in the time-capsule?
* What did you predict for the future?

Convey fun, *fun, FUN!* Trigger memories and encourage your classmates to wonder about "so-and-so."

Send out the "last chance" mailer approximately one month prior to your final deadline. (See sample on next two pages.)

Your goal: Get people to commit *now!*

~ ~

Sample "Last Chance" Mailer Front

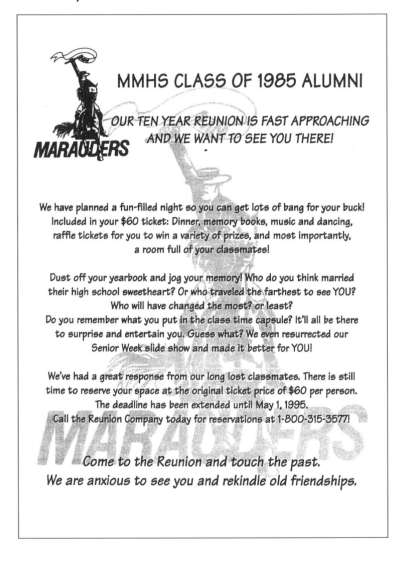

MMHS CLASS OF 1985 ALUMNI

*OUR TEN YEAR REUNION IS FAST APPROACHING
AND WE WANT TO SEE YOU THERE!*

MARAUDERS

We have planned a fun-filled night so you can get lots of bang for your buck!
Included in your $60 ticket: Dinner, memory books, music and dancing,
raffle tickets for you to win a variety of prizes, and most importantly,
a room full of your classmates!

Dust off your yearbook and jog your memory! Who do you think married
their high school sweetheart? Or who traveled the farthest to see YOU?
Who will have changed the most? or least?
Do you remember what you put in the class time capsule? It'll all be there
to surprise and entertain you. Guess what? We even resurrected our
Senior Week slide show and made it better for YOU!

We've had a great response from our long lost classmates. There is still
time to reserve your space at the original ticket price of $60 per person.
The deadline has been extended until May 1, 1995.
Call the Reunion Company today for reservations at 1-800-315-3577!

*Come to the Reunion and touch the past.
We are anxious to see you and rekindle old friendships.*

Sample "Last Chance" Mailer Back

PICNIC!

Family Picnic on Sunday, May 14, 1995 at Mariner's Point on Mission Bay at 3224 Mariner's Way. Look for us in the eastern section of the park.

Keep the Reunion going! Picnic begins at 11:00am. We'll provide the BBQ but bring your own lunch. There will be activities for kids of all ages! Astro jump, over-the-line, relay races, etc. Great prizes too! Come one, come all!

For more information contact Kirk Van Wagoner **123-555-1111**

COCKTAIL PARTY/"ICE BREAKER"

...to be held Friday night at 7:00 pm in the U.S. Grant Lobby Bar. Come join us for appetizers and a no host bar. Reunite with your friends the night before the big party in a more casual setting!

U.S. Grant Hotel
326 Broadway
Downtown San Diego.

~ ~

Producing Mailers

If you have access to software programs which create graphics, it will make the production of your mailers quite cost-effective. Use readily available resources. Is there an artist in your group? Or perhaps you have a committee member who has computer graphics program who can to design your mailers. Does anyone own or work at a print shop? Take advantage of your committee's talents and resources first. They will be glad to help, after all, they are on the reunion committee.

Another alternative for producing your printed materials is using the desktop publishing services at quick-print shops. These service companies can design and lay out your mailer and provide the printing as well. Always give yourself as much lead time as possible. Ask your vendors for guaranteed completion dates.

Check and double-check camera-ready artwork for errors and omissions before handing it to the printer. He's not responsible for your mistakes! He is only responsible for clean work, using your choice of paper, colors, etc. Clearly indicate your selections when placing your order with the printer.

Depending on the layout of your mailer, you may wish to use a Z-fold which leaves the top third of the printed piece exposed, which immediately attracts the recipient's attention. Verify this request ahead of time and inquire if there is an additional charge for using a Z-fold. Retain a sample of the paper you have chosen for your records. Compare what you receive from your printer with what

~ ~

you ordered. Ask the printer to return all original art, as well as any camera-ready materials. All art belongs to you.

~   ~   ~

Congratulations! You have accomplished a lot. Keep your eyes on the road and don't look back. We hope that you and your classmates are having fun meeting regularly and planning a reunion worth remembering. With the search underway, you are discovering the whereabouts of old friends and surely are anxious to see them in person. But, there is still a lot of organizing to do, so keep the committee focused and enthusiastic about the task at hand. In the upcoming meetings, there is more delegating to be done. In many instances, the tasks will overlap.

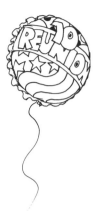

11 - Photographer

~ ~

Not only do classmates want to take home memories of a grand time, but they will want photos to keep alive every moment that transpired so quickly.

In a matter of a few hours, all of those happy, smiling faces captured on film will be but a memory of the greatest reunion ever. Don't risk losing those precious memories for you and your classmates by selecting an amateur photographer or being enticed by a so-called "good deal." The results of not having a real pro at hand to capture the setting, the mood and the people, can make for a bitter ending to an otherwise sweet memory.

~ ~

As reunions are being recognized more and more as an industry, professional photographers who specialize in high school reunions and proms are emerging. These photographers offer a variety of services, which include posed photos, candid photos, memory book production, and occasionally, name badges. If you have the good fortune to find a good photographer, he or she can save you time and expense by preparing the memory book and name badges as part of the service. The photographers also sell reprints of the photos that appear in the memory book to your classmates.

It is wise to interview several photographers before making a choice. If "specialized" reunion photographers are not in your area, check the Yellow Pages for photographers who specialize in dances or weddings. The format of these events is similar to a reunion. Explain to them the basic requirements for both posed photos and candids. The photographer must be willing to offer classmates a way to re-order pictures and assist you in preparing the photos for a memory book.

To ensure full coverage of the event, request that your photographer take pictures in the following manner:

- Posed photos during the check-in/cocktail hour (one to two hours).
- Candid photos throughout the balance of the evening, including the program, mingling, and dancing.

~ ~

Posed Photos

If you recall the way the photographer handled posed photo sessions at your high school dances, then you will see that he follows a similar procedure at the reunion.

Guests receive "photographer cards" at check-in. They fill in their name, mailing address, and use the order form for their selections. The photographer will take the card at the time of the formal posed photo session, use the information for the memory book and mail the order to the address provided. Usually, the photographer can complete the posed photo session during the check-in and cocktail hour.

Photography is usually done in color, but for cost effectiveness, photos in the memory book are are in black and white. Classmates ordering their formal pictures will receive color photography. Discuss this matter with your photographer.

~ ~

Questions to Ask the Photographers

1. Have you photographed dances or reunions before?
2. Do you have a portfolio I could look at?
3. How long have you been in the business?
4. Can you set up for posed and candid photos?
5. How many photographers will be at the event?
6. Do you have a system for re-ordering individual photos?
7. Can you produce a memory book?
8. Do you have a sample memory book? What is included? (i.e., how many pages are dedicated to candids? posed photos? directory?)
9. Will you send them out directly to guests?
10. What is the turnaround time to produce and mail the memory book?
11. Is there a minimum order for memory books?
12. What is the cost?
13. Is a deposit required?
14. Are you the person who will be taking the pictures?
15. Is there a minimum order for photos?
16. Can you provide your own "photographer cards" to hand out at check-in?
17. What extra services are available (i.e., name badges, slide show)?

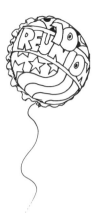

12 - Memory Books

~ ~

Just as reunion party memories begin to fade, copies of the memory book arrive in your mailboxes. Whenever people peruse the pages of the memory book, they can relive the evening at leisure. A memory book or directory is a cherished and worthwhile party favor for you and your guests. It is something that will last forever!

Usually the cost of the memory book is included in the ticket price for attending classmates, and can be offered to absent classmates at a slightly higher rate (Charging more helps to meet the cost of the minimum order requirement — usually of 100 books.) Typically, the cost for a memory book ranges from $8 to $15 per copy. As a committee, you

~ ~

must realize that by offering a memory book for the event, you are committing to some additional work after the reunion. While the photographer provides the photos, it is usually the committee's responsibility to lay out the posed photos and candid shot section for the photographer and submit a directory compiled from the information obtained from the questionnaires.

It can take up to four months to publish the memory book. Three to four weeks after the reunion, the photographer will provide the committee with the photos. When assembly and layout are completed, the committee returns the materials to the printer. After printing, the memory books are mailed to each classmate. We recommend that you have a memory book coordinator assigned before the reunion. It may be appropriate and practical to have your photography coordinator handle the memory book, since they are related tasks.

Some cities have memory book companies and reunion photographers who take on the production of these books from start to finish. For example, in Southern California, some Olan Mills Studios® have a school reunion division that specializes in producing memory books.

You may wish to get several estimates from printers for the purpose of comparing costs before you commit. Give the printer accurate specifications enabling him or her to come up with a realistic bid.

~ ~

Information Required for an Accurate Printer Bid

Let the printer know:

1. How many pieces of photography you intend to use.
2. Number of pages in the book.
3. The kind of paper stock for text and cover you would like to use.
4. If the cover going to be black only, or black plus one or more colors.

A good professional printer will walk you through the process and terminology to help you produce a memorable book for your classmates.

Ask your photographer what he can provide. If you have to assemble the book yourselves, request that your photographer provide you with original studio photos — otherwise the quality of reproducing photography can vary.

Here is a typical format for a memory book:

- Cover. The cover for the book can be designed by the committee. Work on the cover design as soon as possible. You can incorporate the logo used in a mailer or your high school's logo.

- Introduction/Letter from reunion committee. This is the reunion committee's opportunity to recap the highlights of the reunion weekend. It is important to thank everyone for attending and recognize people who made important contributions (besides yourselves) to making the reunion weekend a success. The letter should be no

~ ~

longer than one page. If you have room, you may want to solicit volunteers for the next reunion committee or suggest ideas for the next reunion. The letter should be "signed" by the entire reunion committee. It's also helpful to add committee members' phone numbers, so your classmates can contact you with input or updated addresses.

- Posed photos of classmates and guests with names. The posed photos taken by the photographer are included here. Identify the photos with the classmate's (and guest's) name. Put the classmate's name in capital letters; for example, "Gregory and BARBARA FOSTER Hart."

- Candid photo collage. Create a collage of candid photos taken by the photographer or good quality photos submitted by classmates as well. To ensure a diverse selection of photos for the candids section, consider putting disposable cameras with flash on tables (one per table will suffice). Put labels on the cameras requesting that they be used, but left at the table. Instruct your volunteers to pick them up near the end of the evening. If you select this option, add a couple more pages of "candids" to the memory book, because you'll get a lot of fun photos.

- Classmates We Missed. This section provides a listing of classmates you've "found" but who could not attend. The "classmates we missed" section is prepared using

~ ~

photos solicited in the mailer. Ask the classmates who cannot attend to send in a photo of themselves and their family to be included in the memory book (See Chapter 10, *Producing Effective Mailers*).

- Memorium page. "In Memory Of ... (list their names)." This page is dedicated to the members of your class who have passed on, but remain in your memories.

- Directory. Provide a directory of classmates who attended the event. This is an appropriate place to list name, address, and other information from question-naires, like occupation, children's names and ages. Alphabetize the directory.
  Note: Unless you have permission, do not list names and addresses of classmates who did not attend. There may be a reason why they did not come to the reunion, so do not print their address in the directory unless they send in a questionnaire or give you permission to do so.

- Classmates not located. Reprint your "missing" list, so your classmates can keep looking for those people they want to find for the next Reunion.

- Other Ideas: "Signs of the times." Create a page of noteworthy events from your graduating year. Things to include: Movie Memories: Who won Best Actor? Sports Memories: Who won the World Series? Music Memories: What were the top songs? and Top Story or Happening of the Year. You can compile this

~ ~

information at a library, or the most expedient method would be to use Hallmark's "Remember the Times®" program at its Personalize It! Card Machine®.

Hints

1. Advise your classmates that the photos will not be returned. Not returning the photos will save you time and money.
2. If you want to add additional information on each classmates's occupation, address, or number of children, solicit this information in the questionnaire. Bear in mind: the more elaborate the memory book, the more difficult it is to produce and the more time it takes to complete the project.
3. In case you decide to employ the services of a memory book production company, don't forget to ask if you have to order a minimum number of copies. That will give you an idea whether or not to hire their services.

Photographers typically earn their money from the posed photos ordered by classmates, not from the production of memory books. Photographers offer memory book production services simply because the demand is so high. So, unfortunately, preparing a timely memory book is not usually a high priority for them — set deadlines.

Be certain that you are able to meet the minimum order requirements before you commit. If you think you may end up not meeting the minimum requirement because you don't have enough initial orders, consider producing a

~ ~

reunion directory only. Using the information obtained from the questionnaires and the updated addresses, a committee member could assemble a reunion directory of classmates, or a printing service shop can assist you in formatting the directory.

A memory book is an ideal souvenir for your classmates, but it takes time and effort to create and produce it. Work closely with your photographer in developing a memory book that reflects the quality and the fun of your class reunion.

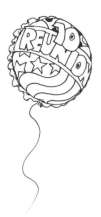

13 - The Event

~ ~

Decorations

Our advice regarding decorations is to *keep it simple.* A simple approach towards decorations does wonders for your budget and your workload, and enables you to focus on the priority aspects of the reunion — like locating classmates!

There are many colorful and attractive ways to decorate a facility for your reunion party. If you have established a theme, your decorations may have to be more elaborate and specific. But, if you do not have a predominant theme, you have a variety of options. Use your committee and

~ ~

classmates as the sources for decorations. Have people donate memorabilia from the high school days: photos for a collage, pompoms as centerpieces, senior prom favors (didn't everyone have "wine" glasses with the school or the prom logo on it?), school newspapers from your senior year, uniforms, etc.

You can use memorabilia as centerpieces and place the rest of them throughout the room. Some committees take memorabilia and create a "memories" section at the reunion as nostalgic reminders of a time and events they all shared. Use easels, corkboards and tables to display the memorabilia in a corner of the room. Even if you opt for other decorations, a memorabilia display from your high school days adds a special touch to the celebration. You'll be amazed what items people have saved and how they jog your memory. Nostalgia is king and fun its royal cohort, and they hold court over a room full of happy revelers — all of which has been arranged by you and your committee. Be certain to label and track loaned memorabilia carefully, and do not put irreplaceable items at risk of being lost or damaged.

With a little brainstorming your committee will come up with great ideas for decorating the facility you have chosen for your reunion. Always consider your resources at hand first. Is anyone on your committee in the catering business or employed by a craft store? They represent great resources for decorating ideas. Craft stores sell vases, silk flowers, confetti, round mirrors (for centerpieces), candles, etc., at reasonable prices, and their staff has great suggestions for do-it-yourself decorations.

~ ~

Another popular, simple and highly festive decorating idea is the use of balloons. Balloons can be used in bunches tied together at various lengths with brilliantly colored ribbons as a centerpiece, or more elaborately crafted into balloon arches with the class year designed into the arch. For more drama and color, fill the ceiling with inflated balloons in the school colors, or place them in bunches throughout the room, as you would use bouquets of flowers. Depending on your application, there are companies that specialize in decorating with balloons. It will cost you to use their expertise, but it doesn't cost anything to ask them for a bid (and ideas)! A festive gathering like a reunion should be *colorful.* For more color, utilize confetti, jelly beans or candy kisses sprinkled around your main centerpiece.

Fresh flowers add a beautiful touch to any event, but they also make pretty stiff demands on your budget. Ask your committee how important decorations are? If you would like to use some flowers, look at the alternatives to huge bouquets and fancy centerpieces.

You can create charming centerpieces using fresh-cut flowers and simple containers. Fashion an "English bouquet" with flowers and rent or purchase vases from a florist. An English bouquet is a small arrangement of cut flowers in a vase without ornamental greenery or baby's breath. If you have access to wholesale flowers, a small bouquet on each table can be as economical as a balloon centerpiece.

~ ~

Selecting your decorations is only half the battle — you have to do the work of hanging, nailing, tacking, draping, placing and executing your ideas. Your committee chairperson can do all the negotiating and purchasing and can even rally the committee to do pre-reunion assembling, but we encourage you to find volunteers to place the decorations the day of the event.

I know, you will want to supervise and that is understandable, but it goes without saying that the entire committee will prefer not to be inflating balloons an hour before the reunion. It is best to recruit volunteers. (How about the same group who is going to work the check-in? Or volunteers from the graduating class behind yours? Or hire hotel staff to assist you with decorating the room.) Prepare as many of the decorations as early as possible (obviously you can't inflate balloons days in advance). Ask the hotel or facility staff how early in the day you can set up for the event.

Hint

If you do set up several hours before the event, make sure the room is supervised or locked until you are ready to use it.

Name Badges

There is a variety of name badges available — anything from the "Hi, My Name Is … " label to custom-made photo badges. In perusing a local office supply store, you will find all kinds of name badges: There are the basic

~ ~

sticky labels — write your own name or use computer generated lettering. Office supply stores offer name badges such as the hanging neck badge, pin-style or clip-style made of clear plastic.

However, the custom-made photo name badge which includes the graduation photo and name is the most popular reunion name badge.

"Our name badges had our graduation photos on them. It was fun to compare looks," said Michael Broyles from Los Gatos High School of his 10-year reunion. Similarly, The Reunion Company in Redlands, California always provides photo name badges. "People really appreciate the photo badges — they are perfect ice-breakers and set a fun mood for the reunion."

One way of acquiring graduation photos is to get color or laser copies of yearbook pages. Remember to copy pages with faculty members attending the reunion. Then, cut out each individual photo and affix it to cardstock. Add the classmate's full name in *bold* lettering. If the woman has changed her name, add her last name used in high school in parentheses or underline it — such as, "TIFFANY (BROWN) SUVER" or "TIFFANY <u>BROWN</u> SUVER."

There are different ways to create the actual badge. One method used by The Reunion Company is a button machine. Committees can rent a button machine to create a high-quality, sturdy badge. As The Reunion Company noted, "Some classmates don't like the stick pin from the button, so sometimes we laminate the cardstock and add a velcro strip to the back. It's simply a matter of preference."

~ ~

In selecting either method, allow yourselves at least ten hours to assemble the number of badges for your party.

It is important to monitor your response cut-off date to allow yourselves enough time to prepare the photo badges. Whenever possible, faculty members who have yearbook pictures should receive photo badges. Persons who miss the deadline, non-alumni guests, and walk-ups cannot receive custom badges. Keep a box of sticky labels handy for those extra guests at check-in time. Photo badges are fun and classmates are delighted with them, but don't spend the last moment before the party making them for last-minute arrivals.

Check-In

Ready, Set, Go! The check-in point is the first stop for classmates when they arrive at the reunion. Words to live by when you set up the check-in station are *organized* and *efficient.*

Organize a smooth and quick check-in procedure. Your guests will be anxious to get on with the party, and your work should be over, so you don't want to have to worry about anything at this point. It's time for you to celebrate the success of your endeavor.

We suggest that you recruit "other" people to work at your check-in table. Ask brothers or sisters or find people from the reunion committee of the class behind you — surely they will be interested in gathering ideas from your event. This way you and your committee members are free to enjoy all your hard work. Your attention to the smallest detail *before* the event will make it smooth sailing and you will be able to truly enjoy the event.

After observing over 2,000 reunions, a reunion photographer offers the following advice, "Unlike other social events, people attending a reunion are more anxious to meet up with the other guests — their classmates. Often, these eager party-goers arrive not just on time, but an hour or more before the formal hour, clustering about, waiting to be checked in. If your event is planned to begin at 6:30 p.m., have your reception table set up for check-in at least half an hour earlier."

The check-in period usually lasts approximately one and a half hours. During that time, classmates can have their posed photos taken and enjoy the cocktail hour. The check-in station should be comprised of a long table or series of tables so that your helpers can process several lines at once.

When you set up the check-in station, provide four lines for pre-registered, pre-paid guests. Divide these lines by the alphabet (A-F, G-L, M-R, S-Z). Have a check-off list for each alphabetized group. At check-in, each pre-registered classmate will receive an envelope with his or her name badge, guest's name badge, photographer's card, schedule of events and any other handouts — such as, raffle tickets, drink coupons, a questionnaire (awards ceremony categories).

Assemble the registration packets before the event. That means name badges, schedule of event flyer/brochure, and raffle tickets must be prepared weeks in advance. Give yourself enough time to prepare the packets and review the list (over and over) again to check for omissions. Each packet should have the classmates name on the front and be filed alphabetically.

Provide your volunteers with extra pens and pencils, envelopes and blank name badges. Keep a good supply of all the materials that are included in the registration package. Inevitably, someone is going to miss, misplace or lose something from the envelope's contents. It saves time and headaches if you can provide the missing material instantly.

Set up one line for "Walk-Ups" or "Pay-at-the-Door" guests. Anticipate approximately 20–30 walk-up guests, and include at least half that number in your guarantee to the caterer.

A surprised reunion committee for Redlands High School Class of 1984 experienced an influx of 100 walk-up guests at their reunion in Palm Springs. Fortunately, the committee gauged liberally and was able to accommodate seventy walk-up guests for the entire event. Instead of turning away the remaining thirty, a resourceful reunion organizer asked them to pay half price for their tickets, dine at the hotel restaurant and and join the reunion party after dinner was served. It was a good solution for the guests, but the check-in staff was overwhelmed. So be prepared for everything!

We assure you that you will need a separate line for walk-ups because the check-in process is more lengthy for unexpected guests.

First, welcome your walk-up guest with a happy "aren't-you-glad-you-decided-to-attend" smile; then collect the ticket money.

~ ~

Hint

Accept cash only at the event. Have change available. This is an opportune time for a bad check to slip through. Ask the classmate who wants to write a check to cash his check at the hotel desk or look for an Automatic Teller Machine. Have a cash box with change handy. The more organized and efficient you are, the smoother the event.

As we suggested earlier, walk- up guests are required to pay the full ticket price in cash. It is quite possible that you will collect over $1,000 at the door. Be sure you have a responsible person at the walk-up table and a safe place for stashing the money after check-in. If your party is at a hotel, place your cash box in the hotel safe. Take the time to secure your loot before the party gets rolling.

Ask the walk-up guests to fill out a questionnaire similar to the one pre-registered classmates submitted. Remember to incorporate their answers into your program and awards ceremony. Prepare name tags for your classmate and guests. Since there won't be time to assemble a photo badge for a walk up guest, use the extra sticky labels. Finally, provide an envelope with additional hand-outs — raffle tickets or a schedule of events and/or the reunion program.

~ ~

Important Tips

1. Insist your check-in volunteers greet every guest with the friendliest welcome as they arrive. You worked hard to find them — their presence is appreciated, so convey this appreciation at the first encounter. Make the classmates feel that their being there is just what everyone has waited for and that they are the icing on the cake!

2. Ask your volunteers to explain the handouts briefly. If you are enclosing a raffle ticket, have its purpose explained. If there are photographer's cards, inform the guests to fill them out, and return them to the photographer at the time their posed photos are taken for the memory book. Urge the walk-ups to have their photos taken right away.

For a festive and nostalgic touch that immediately brings back memories, include a piece of school memorabilia in the check-in packet. Use your high school logo or reunion slogan to decorate the buttons or ribbons you hand out. I vividly remember how popular special game ribbons and buttons were at home football games. We would proudly wear our *Trap the Tigers* ribbons. We had a new ribbon for every game. Mementos like that created camaraderie and excitement in those days, and are sure to bring out the same feelings and reactions at your reunion.

~ ~

After-Dinner Program

The program you have created is the evening's after-dinner entertainment — just before the dancing begins and lasting no longer than one hour. Your guests will want to make the most of visiting with each other, so you will notice they have a short attention span.

A surefire way to make the program memorable is to select an energetic and humorous master of ceremony — somebody who has something for everybody, and who can tease a laugh out of a rock. You're looking for the kind of person who would have been an "entertainer."

Nori Patrick from Palm Springs High School, '83 talked about the program at her 10-year reunion. "The program was amazing. The emcees were hilarious, and our slide show brought back many wonderful memories. It was a terrific evening."

Sometimes a committee member acts as the emcee for the evening. This is appropriate, but not necessary. If you have one or several classmates you recall as being funny and charismatic, ask them if they would be interested in the job. You can also solicit for emcees in your mailers. Remember, the most important attributes of your master(s) of ceremonies should be:

- Willing to entertain.
- Exudes enthusiasm.
- A talent for laughter.
- An ease of presence.
- A free spirit.
- Able to build rapport easily.

~ ~

Hint

Encourage several individuals to be master of ceremony and share the job. Let them run with it!

A Sample Program May Look Like This

It is helpful to distribute a written version of the program among your guests so they can follow what's going on.

1. Introduction of the Committee. After all, you've put a lot of heart and soul into planning this reunion. Recognize yourselves! One committee member from Palm Springs High School was most surprised at the reunion by "the warmth and good feelings the committee received for organizing the event."

2. Recognize special guests. Recognize the teachers, advisors, and principals in attendance. Make special note of how they contributed to your high school experience. This is also a good time to thank all of your volunteers by name!

3. Awards. Using the questionnaire information (see sample questionnaire in Chapter 10, *Producing Effective Mailers*), you may choose to hand out prizes for various categories:
   • Farthest distance traveled to attend.
   • Most kids.
   • Best golf score.
   • Most (or least!) hair.

~ ~

- Married the longest.
- Married high school sweetheart.
- Most unique job or career.
- Most recent newly-weds.

Your prizes can be gags or modest gifts:
- Bottles of wine or champagne.
- Gift certificates.
- Movie tickets.
- Bus ticket to the next reunion.
- Olan Mills® Picture Package for the "most children" award.
- Theme park admission tickets.
- Restaurant gift certificate.

4. Raffle. If you have a generous supply of donated prizes or centerpieces that can be raffled, you may want to hold a raffle during the program. We have already mentioned that raffle tickets can be placed in the check-in packages. If you are holding a fundraising raffle, solicit participants or pick the winner at this time.

5. Slide show. As mentioned before, the slide show is usually the highlight of the program. (See Chapter 13, *The Event*, "Slide Show/Video Presentation" Section.)

6. Information on picnic and other activities. Inform your guest about the time, the location and the cost, if any, of each activity.

~ ~

7. Icebreakers and interactive ideas. If you have a captive audience, it's fun to get the group mingling as a whole, because it is typical for cliques to re-emerge as people find each other and spend the whole evening catching up. But, because the passage of time finds us on common ground with more of our classmates, it's exciting to have an icebreaker to get everyone reacquainted. Your master of ceremonies can orchestrate something as simple as "musical chairs" to get the group laughing and moving around! If you have a school teacher in the group, certainly you can come up with a few 5-10 minute games to create interaction.

Kimberly Walther from Mira Mesa High School in San Diego shared: "Our emcee was amazing. He planned an icebreaker game that literally got everyone involved. Every classmate received a piece of paper naming an 'old' popular TV show, such as M.A.S.H. or Happy Days. We had to find the other people with the same show. The whole group was milling about, singing show-tunes and looking for one another. Once assembled, the groups had to sing the show's theme song. The best rendition won drink coupons. It was a great incentive, but our group couldn't remember the words to "Scooby-Doo."

Consider creating a high school trivia game with prizes or raffle tickets for correct answers. This is a great way to get the group involved (and listening). Trivia questions could be:

- Who did our football team play in the 1984 championship game?

~ ~

- What musical group won the Air Band Contest our senior year?
- Who was our valedictorian?
- What was the theme song for the prom?
- Who jumped into Mission Bay at our senior luncheon?

Flip through your yearbook to jog your memories and get ideas for questions. Try to include varied questions so many classmates can participate.

Dating Game: *A high school in Southern California reenacted the ever-popular show "The Dating Game®" at their ten-year reunion. Several committee members recalled coordinating the game in high school between their school and the "rival" high school. Since it had been such a success in high school, they decided it would be a fun (and possibly promising) event at their reunion. The stage was set and the disc jockey even had the theme song on hand. The participants were willing and less inhibited than they were in high school!*

Slide Show/Video Presentation

The presentation of a slide show makes a big splash at any event. A montage of pictures set to music is a great addition to your reunion program and really takes your guests on a trip down memory lane. Even if your class has a slide show preserved from your senior year, in the invitation, ask classmates to send in photos from their high school years to include in the show.

~ ~

If you prefer to have a professional put your slide show together, you have several choices. Your photographer may be able to convert photos submitted by classmates into slides and place them into a carousel and add music to the presentation. Some full-service photo finishing studios can also do the job. A videographer can put your slides and photos together on tape with music. This medium lends itself well for adding all sorts of special effects, although it is a more costly process. Check your budget and see what money you have available.

In most instances, you provide the videographer with a list of songs which the producer then blends with the photos for an effective show. It's always fun to select music with lyrics that are upbeat, or to choose melodies specifically related to your own high school era. Get the crowd involved! They'll clap to the beat of the tunes, they'll shriek with laughter when photos of themselves from high school appear on the screen.

Confirm with the management of your selected facility that appropriate audio/visual equipment is available. Some facilities do not have equipment and you will have to rent what you need. Establish rental prices prior to producing your slide show/video. Everything comes out of your budget for the event and it helps to know where your money is going.

~ ~

Music and Entertainment

There is nothing like a song — a special slow dance to linger on in one's memory and conjure up the past. It never fails that, when I hear Led Zeppelin's *Stairway to Heaven,* a smile crosses my face. We all remember the anxiety and insecurity that flooded us before that special someone would ask us to dance. And then came that rush of pride (and relief) when he came, and he asked, and we danced.

Songs from your high school days bring their own magic for that extra touch to the party. While you are spending hours creating a nostalgic environment for your guests, the easiest way to trigger fond memories is to hire a disc jockey or a band to resurrect all the popular songs from your high school years. The dance floor will be packed all night long.

The cost for a disc jockey and a band differ greatly — sometimes as much as $1,500. Considering your budget and the ticket price, a band may not be a realistic option. However, disc jockeys provide an excellent service, create the mood you want and present your requests for songs in their original version. You will hear the songs you remember.

Hints

Read each contract carefully, and be aware of special requirements before signing your name on the dotted line. For instance, many vendors require a cashier's check the night of the event. If you agree to their special requests, make arrangements ahead of time.

~ ~

Provide your band or DJ with a schedule of events for the evening. They can make announcements throughout the evening for dinner, the start of the program and the awards ceremony.

Set up a schedule of events, so that the evening can progress without your constant attention. After all, the committee members will get caught up in the excitement as well and may lose track of time. Assign a contact person from the committee to answer any questions your entertainer(s) may have.

Questions to Ask Your Entertainers

1. Have you ever entertained at a high school reunion?
2. Will you accept requests for songs?
3. Can you make announcements throughout the evening?
4. What is your fee for an evening? What are the terms of payment?
5. Do you want a deposit? How much? Is the deposit refundable?
6. Do you have special set-up requirements?
7. How often do you take a break? For how long?
8. Do you want dinner? When do you take a dinner break?
9. How far in advance will you want to set up?

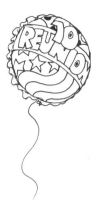

Post-Reunion Tasks and Suggestions

~ ~

Reunion Recap

First of all, revel in your success. Have a follow-up committee meeting, or party to review the event. This is an important follow-up meeting, so tempt your committee with a treat. If you have money left from the reunion fund, invite them to a dinner meeting.

At the wrap-up:
1. Review the highlights of the reunion and discuss the things you'd like to change for the next one. Perhaps

~ ~

you will want a longer cut-off time, a more exciting menu, additional staff for the event, different mailers or a different location. Perhaps you have some classmates who volunteered to help with the next one. Whatever the feedback, take notes. They'll come in handy when it's time to plan another reunion. And what better way to improve on the next event than to learn from the mistakes and the successes of the last one. Whether it will be your job or someone else's, the next committee members will appreciate the recommendations and suggestions they inherited from their predecessor.

2. Delegate future reunion responsibilities to a committee member. Choose this volunteer carefully, since you will be entrusting him or her with all the updated lists, the reunion fund bank account, the slide show, and all the things that have accumulated, from memorabilia to paperwork.

3. Budget review. Ask your money manager to provide a summary of reunion expenses. Was the budget realistic? Can some areas of spending be improved for next time? And, most importantly, are we in the black? If you are faced with outstanding bills, start thinking about fundraising ideas.

~ ~

Fundraisers

A fundraiser is absolutely necessary if you have an outstanding debt after the event. (See Chapter 6, *Meeting #2*, "Fundraising" Section for ideas.) If you foresee budget problems immediately before the reunion party, organize a raffle at the event or announce future fundraising plans. Ask someone to spearhead the fundraiser.

Memory Book

The photographer will deliver the photographs within three to four weeks. Make sure the memory book coordinator and committee are prepared to dig right in and get the job done. Set dates for completion. Your classmates will be eagerly awaiting their memory books. Be prepared for phone calls from "extra-anxious" people. This should spur you on to get it done. (See also Chapter 12, *Memory Books.*)

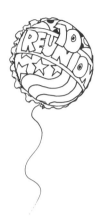

Epilogue

~ ~

You've done it ! You accomplished what you set out to do. You remembered what it was you wanted your guests to take with them from the party, and you gave it to them. They have left behind their gratitude for a weekend well-spent. It was an event worthy of making fond, new memories — nostalgic, heart-warming and soul-filling. Your guests left with a generous doggie-bag full of extra joy and left-over good feelings. They met old friends and found new ones — even a romance or two may have blushed into life.

You gave the past a future, and you created a faithful following for the next time — to park the kids, put the dog in the kennel, buy a party dress, pack the bags and come to the next reunion. You paved the way for continuing good relationships, more friendly camaraderie and a sense of belonging — people have re-established roots and bonds — bonds that go back a decade and more.

While you have set a fine example for the next committee for planning another reunion, you have also proven that you and your committee are a hard act to follow. With all this hectic activity, all this careful planning, looking after the smallest details, soothing ruffled feathers, making deals with hotels and support services, holding meetings and planning sessions, pulling it all together — did you not have a lot of fun?

Of course, you did. We know you did!

See you at the next reunion. We'll be there.

~ ~

Things to Remember

Remember to:…

- … Be sure your high school and local newspapers have your name, the date and location of your reunion.

- … Give your committee and classmates as much time as possible to plan your reunion — 9 to 12 months minimum.

- … Select a location that is easy to get to and affordable, yet has a great atmosphere.

- … Reserve sleeping rooms for out-of-town classmates, if possible.

- … Try every method possible for locating lost classmates.

- … Invest time planning an interesting and entertaining program for your reunion evening.

- … Try everything possible to keep the cost down.

- … Get everything in writing from all your vendors, hotel, entertainers and photographer.

~ ~

Things to Remember (cont'd.)
Remember to:...

- ... Call all your vendors the week before the reunion and confirm every detail.

- ... Create festive centerpieces and room decorations.

- ... You can't please everyone. There will always be people who complain, but most of your classmates will be thrilled that someone has taken the time and effort to plan the reunion.

- ... It is the people who make the party and your goal above all else is to have fun.

- ... Be realistic when estimating attendance. Don't base your attendance on one-half of the size of your class plus dates. Your total attendance (including dates) will be 30 to 35 percent of your class size.

- ... Your main goal is to get as many classmates as possible to attend. Don't try to be too ambitious or unique in planning this once-every-five- or ten-year event.

~ ~

Things to Remember (cont'd.)
Remember to:....

- You are the customer. Don't be pressured by vendors. Ask a lot of questions and remember you can always say no.

- Invite faculty.

- Acknowledge those who have passed on.

- Have a great time!

Index

~ ~

~ ~

~ ~

~ ~

~ ~

~ ~

Notes

Notes

Notes

Notes

Notes

To order:

Planning Your High School Reunion

Please send ____ cop(ies) at $14.95 each; plus $3.50 shipping and handling for the first book, $2 for each additional book.

Enclosed is my check or money order for $_____

or [ ] Visa [ ] MasterCard

_____ Exp. Date _____

Signature _____

Phone _____

Name _____

Street Address_____

City _____

State _____ Zip _____

(Advise if recipient and mailing address is different from above.)

Return this order form to:
Montage Publishing
13501 100th Avenue N.E., Suite 5047
Kirkland, WA 98034

**For credit card orders, call toll free:
1-800-315-3577**